University of Sunderland
University Library Services

Renew and manage your account onlir
library.sunderland.ac.uk
Tel: (0191) 5153691
Facebook/UniOfSunLib
Twitter/UniOfSunLib

FOUR WEEK LOAN
The Murray Library

Please return on or before the date shown below.
Fines will be charged for all late returns.

ιe most
ssment,
ιis case
ven the
school
letailed
aw, and
les, the
spiring

Teacher

he City
r Peace

CASE STUDIES ON SAFETY, BULLYING, AND SOCIAL MEDIA IN SCHOOLS

CURRENT ISSUES IN EDUCATIONAL LEADERSHIP

Laura Trujillo-Jenks
Kenneth Jenks

Routledge
Taylor & Francis Group

NEW YORK AND LONDON

First published 2016
by Routledge
711 Third Avenue, New York, NY 10017

and by Routledge
2 Park Square, Milton Park, Abingdon, Oxon, OX14 4RN

Routledge is an imprint of the Taylor & Francis Group, an informa business

© 2016 Taylor & Francis

Library of Congress Cataloging in Publication Data
A catalog record for this book has been requested

ISBN: 978-1-138-91183-3 (hbk)
ISBN: 978-1-138-91184-0 (pbk)
ISBN: 978-1-315-69232-6 (ebk)

Typeset in New Baskerville
by HWA Text and Data Management, London

MIX
Paper from
responsible sources
FSC   FSC® C013056
www.fsc.org

Printed and bound in Great Britain by
TJ International Ltd, Padstow, Cornwall

We dedicate this book on behalf of our children:
Lyle, Sean, Alexandria, and Jordan.

We also dedicate this book to all educators and peace officers who work
tirelessly at making schools a safe, orderly, and happy place to be!

Contents

Preface

This book was written for pre-service and current teachers and administrators. We wanted to share our knowledge gained from years of experience to help you guide your students to success. For current educators, we believe this book can be used as a preventative exercise in ensuring your campus is as safe, orderly, and happy as possible. It can be used in your professional development, faculty meetings, or book study. It allows for provocative discussions and helps you create plans of action. For pre-service educators, the use of case studies allows you to practice applying knowledge to your own school contexts.

HOW TO USE THIS BOOK

Although the stories in this book have been embellished or combined at times, the situations presented in these case studies have occurred in real schools. The names of persons and schools involved have been changed, and none of the names used in this book refer to actual people or schools. We suggest that as you read each case study, you make notes or a chart or list of the different variables and consider the problems posed in each case by plotting your data. An example of plotting information for Chapter 11 could look like:

Persons in Case Study

Becca
Carter

Actions of Person

Becca

1 Obsessed with Carter
2 Constant texts

Outcomes for that Person

Becca

1 Being pushed away by Carter
2 Has become intrusive and emotional

Other Information

Becca

1 Captain of girl's basketball team
2 Likeable student by peers and teachers

HOW THIS BOOK IS ORGANIZED

Through case studies and mini case studies, this book simulates events that occur on a school campus and within a school community. The first eleven chapters are divided into three sections each, presenting situations and queries concerning a relevant, real, and timely issue that affects public education. After reading each case, you can assess what the best course of action might be when considering the elements of the case.

The first section, *The Case* will focus on a certain event during a specified time frame. A series of characters will be introduced, along with pertinent information needed to understand why the characters behave as they do. Demographics of the school, community, student population, and school district may be provided to help enhance the understanding of the case. As you read the case, a problem will emerge, and you must address and develop a data-driven decision based on the facts presented. Think: *If this happened on my campus, what would I do?* Unfortunately, some readers may find that some of these cases, or some version of them, have occurred on their campus; our hope would be that revisiting and discussing the event might help prevent similar ones in the future.

Each case study presents layer upon layer of issues, crises, and events. You can decide to tackle all of the layers at once, or concentrate on one layer at a time, leaving the other layers for another reading. The beauty of each case study is that each time you read the case study, you will find yet another layer to work through and discuss. And, because so many topics are being addressed in one case study, you may decide to focus on one topic at a time.

The second section of each chapter is *What Else Do I Need to Know?* After each case, supportive information and a brief literature review will follow. In all chapters, insight from experience from the authors will be given. Undoubtedly, this section provides more information for you to consider before coming to a professional conclusion on how to address the case. Finally, further information on the topic may be given through websites and other resources at the end of this section and/or in the reference section.

The *No Consequence Zone (NCZ)* is the last section of each chapter, which helps you think about possible solutions to the issues presented. You can consider these cases and make decisions without having to worry about the real ramifications such decisions may have. Further, if a decision you have made isn't the best one, then you can review that decision and try again without any consequence. Case studies and the NCZ are the perfect way to learn and to practice being a successful educator.

The final chapter contains mini case studies for the educator on the go. Sometimes, there may not be an hour to discuss one of the other case studies, which is why the mini case studies are so helpful. You can choose from a variety of different topics, like *Curriculum, Instruction, Attendance, Special Populations, Educator Contracts, Ethics, Academic Freedom, Speech Rights of Educators, Student Code of Conduct, Speech Rights of Students, Religion on Campus, Privacy, Liability and Immunity,* and spend between 5–10 minutes discussing a quick solution and plan of action.

A NOTE ABOUT TERMINOLOGY

In order to understand some of the language used in this book, a list of words with synonyms are listed below. Because not every school shares the same vernacular, please refer to this list as needed.

- Assistant Principal will always be denoted as AP. An assistant principal is akin to a vice principal.
- Staff will always refer to every employee on a campus, which will include teachers, teacher aides, secretaries, cafeteria cooks, administrators, etc.
- When discussing the evaluation or appraisal of a teacher, a walk-thru may be discussed. A walk-thru is when an administrator spends 3–15 minutes observing a teacher, gaining a quick snapshot of what is occurring in the classroom.
- Skilled teachers are what classification the majority of teachers fit into. Skilled teachers are proficient and are seen as effective and successful.
- An ARD/IEP is a meeting that is held for a student in special education. In some states, the term Admission, Review, and Dismissal (ARD) is

used instead of the more common term Individualized Education Plan (IEP) when referring to a student's annual meeting.

- The School Board/Board of Trustees is the governing body of a school district. They approve and pass the policies that must be followed by all educators within a school district.
- Student Code of Conduct or SCOC is the "law of the land" for students in a school district and on a school campus. It is what all students should abide by and all educators should follow when disciplining students.
- Penal Code and Criminal Code are synonymous throughout this book. Both refer to the laws or statutes in each state that law enforcement and the judicial system uphold. Convictions for violations of these codes could result in jail/prison time, fines, or both.

In short, the best use for this book is to read each case study and discuss the details and the additional information provided. Using this book in an education course or on a school campus will enhance the learning of educators. The case studies are application-based activities that simulate real circumstances and problems that face educators today. This book provides educators with the tools to apply federal, state, and local laws/codes/policies to find safe and plausible outcomes.

Enjoy learning and becoming an effective and successful educator!

I Am the Superintendent's Wife!

When a new administrator begins working on a campus, getting to know its culture is a top priority. To succeed in the job and to keep it, an administrator must understand the culture, which includes, among other things, the shared beliefs, values, history, and traditions of the campus and its demographics, leadership hierarchy, and ways of doing things. In the case study presented in this chapter, surviving in his position becomes a concern for a new assistant principal assigned to evaluate the teaching performance of the district superintendent's wife. In fact, many educators and students at the school have mere survival as their main goal when interacting with this teacher, who has more clout than she should have.

If a practice that does not promote success on a campus becomes the norm, educators must work together to change that practice. When leaders, however, such as the principal, the superintendent, and the board of trustees support the practice, educators are likely to feel uncomfortable about implementing or even suggesting a change. Allowing someone to follow his/her own rules and to ignore the needs of the campus as a whole affects all who work with his/her, and both their morale and the campus culture suffer. So this thorny problem must be addressed.

THE CASE

The Superintendent's Wife

"Don't you know who I am? I am the superintendent's wife, and I can make your life hell." These words are often repeated by Mrs. Albert when she is talking with high school students in her family and consumer science course. She delights in reminding students, parents, and colleagues that her husband is the district's superintendent, and that if she does not like you, she will make sure you are dealt with in the most demeaning manner. For example, a fellow family and consumer science teacher had decorated the bulletin board in her classroom with Valentine hearts one day in February. When Mrs. Albert walked into the room, she yelled, "What the hell are all these hearts doing on your bulletin board? This doesn't look like a family science classroom. This looks like a kindergarten classroom. Someone as stupid as you just might not have a job after today, once Dr. Albert hears about this!"

Mrs. Albert has been working in the Paradise View School District for twenty-five years, ever since she and her husband moved to the city of Paradise View when he was hired as an assistant superintendent for the district. After eight years in that position, Dr. Albert was promoted to associate superintendent, and five years later he became the superintendent. When Dr. Albert first came to the district, the school board was very excited to welcome him to Paradise View and even found a position for Mrs. Albert as a home economics teacher. Dr. Albert was revered because he was a strong leader who was seen as fair and because he knew how to save money for the school district.

Mrs. Albert was also revered when she first started teaching at Paradise View High School. Students always wanted to take her home economics class, which always had a waiting list. As the years passed, however, newer and younger teachers were being hired, becoming the students' favorite teachers, and a jealous Mrs. Albert felt that they might be popular but not as knowledgeable or experienced as she. She began to resent the newer teachers and started to bring up her husband's position to threaten people and coerce them to do things her way.

Through the years, students, parents, and other teachers have lodged many complaints about Mrs. Albert's behavior. They faulted her for screaming at her students and using profanity when she did so, and they observed that she rarely was actually in the classroom teaching while students were there. Instead, she could be found in her office on the phone or at her computer. When parents requested a parent-teacher conference, Mrs. Albert always refused and was never available. When the parents would complain to the principal, Mr. Waned would support Mrs. Albert and would conduct his own parent-teacher conference on her behalf.

Some parents took their complaints further, to the superintendent and the school board, yet they never received a satisfactory response. Both the superintendent and the school board backed Mr. Waned and Mrs. Albert, even stating that when students do not comply with the Student Code of Conduct or classroom expectations, teachers must keep order and employ whatever means necessary for students to learn. When parents and students explained that no learning was occurring in Mrs. Albert's classroom, the superintendent and school board members would remind them that Mrs. Albert was a teacher with a wealth of knowledge. If students refused to learn, they said, that simply proved the students' lack of responsibility and motivation and did not reflect badly on Mrs. Albert. Thus, these students, parents, and teachers did not feel supported by these leaders, and they hoped that soon the superintendent and the principal, along with the school board, would be replaced. Conversely, there were parents and students that adored Mrs. Albert and felt because of her, students could be very successful in her class and in life.

The Principal and the Assistant Principal

Mr. Waned has been at Paradise View High School (PVHS) for seventeen years. He was first the head coach for eleven years and then an assistant principal (AP) for one year, and he has been the principal for the past five years. Before coming to Paradise View, he worked for two years with Superintendent Albert in a nearby school district as an assistant coach, and Dr. Albert recruited him to be the head coach at PVHS. Mr. Waned and Dr. Albert have grown very close throughout the years, even keeping a standing weekend tee time at the local country club.

PVHS is a large school, and it has had an influx of students during the past several years, prompting the school board to approve a third AP position; a Mr. Shouse filled this new position. Mr. Shouse had been an English teacher at another high school, where he was well liked and skillful at motivating students. His students always passed the state standardized exams with high scores, and he frequently worked with his school administration to help other teachers to achieve similar success with their students. This year is Mr. Shouse's sixth year in education, and this is his first job as an AP.

When the other APs at PVHS administrators learned that Mr. Shouse was being assigned to their campus, they were elated because they could pass on all supervisory responsibilities concerning Mrs. Albert to the "new guy," including observation of her classroom and evaluation of her teaching. Mr. Shouse heard the rumors about Mrs. Albert, and although he decided that he would be cautious, he has maintained a positive attitude when interacting with her. Mr. Shouse has made several observations, both informal and formal, in Mrs. Albert's classroom. He observed typical classroom teaching and learning behaviors, but he also observed Mrs. Albert do some things that alarmed him, such as yelling at students without provocation, ignoring students repeatedly when they had questions, catering to one or two favorite students for an entire class period, and leaving her classroom ten minutes before the period ended and not returning until the next class started. When Mr. Shouse approached Mrs. Albert about his concerns, she promptly told him, "If you make trouble for me, you should watch your back. And if you don't stop coming into my classroom to check up on me, you won't like the consequences."

Mr. Shouse wanted to be fair to Mrs. Albert, and he needed to confirm how what he observed affected the students. During lunch duty one day, he approached a group of students and asked how they liked taking home economics. The reviews were mixed but, overall, the students shared that although Mrs. Albert could be a witch at times, they learned neat stuff about cooking and preparing meals. No glaring abuse was spoken of.

Mr. Shouse went to Mr. Waned to brief him on Mrs. Albert and to get guidance on how to work with her, but the principal was not in his office. He then went to the other two assistant principals and asked them if they had any tips on how to handle what he observed in Mrs. Albert's classroom. They told him since this was his first year as an AP, he needed to avoid making any trouble for himself, or he would find himself black-balled. They also informed him that going to Mr. Waned would not help his case and that he would be told that Superintendent Albert and the school board would always back his support of Mrs. Albert, and they would support her before supporting anyone else.

The New Student

When her mother's job was transferred to the predominantly Caucasian and Hispanic community of Paradise View, Lauren Kenny, a freshman of Asian origin, enrolled at PVHS. At her previous school, Lauren excelled in academics, and her teachers loved her good manners and scholarly discipline. She was a straight-A student and was musically inclined, playing the violin. At PVHS, she joined the orchestra and the drama club and quickly made friends. She felt that the move to PVHS would prove to be a good one.

Lauren was assigned to a family and consumer science class with Mrs. Albert. Lauren had not heard anything one way or the other about Mrs. Albert, so she was looking forward to taking the class. At first, Lauren sat quietly in the front of the class and eagerly waited to learn the day's lesson. What she found on most days, however, was that she and her classmates were instructed to read certain pages of the course textbook and answer a series of questions. She longed to learn how to cook and budget for different meals in a household, but those days were few and far between. What Lauren did realize was that Mrs. Albert may not be the best teacher, but as long as she stayed out of her way, she would survive the semester.

The time to cook came one Friday, and Lauren was excited. She had her cooking area ready with the needed ingredients and pans, and her recipe was upright in the recipe stand. As she was preparing to begin mixing her ingredients, Mrs. Albert walked by and hit her on the head with a wooden spoon, growling, "Don't start yet! Wait for me to give the signal!" The hit on the head was painful and Lauren was shocked and hurt by this action. She kept to herself for the rest of the class and decided to just let it go and just pray for the semester to end.

During lunch, Mr. Waned made small talk with Lauren and her friends as they waited in the lunch line. He asked how they liked their classes and which class was their favorite. Lauren told how her favorite was orchestra and her least favorite was home economics. When Mr. Waned pushed Lauren for more information, she flippantly stated, "You know, unstable people shouldn't be teaching especially when they hit kids on the head with a wooden spoon!" and then went to grab her food.

Mr. Waned did not know what to make of the comment, so he decided to go and observe Mrs. Albert's class again. As he approached her room, he heard her state to a student, "Don't mess with me, because my husband is the superintendent. So it doesn't matter if you tell your parent or not—nothing will happen to me. But dire things may happen to you." When Mr. Waned walked in the classroom, he saw Mrs. Albert walking away from a shaken Lauren.

Mr. Shouse was nervous about how to address this situation. When he went to speak to Mrs. Albert after class about what he heard and observed, she snapped, "You need to learn your place at this school and know that you never bother me with trivial dialogue!" She then walked away and slammed her office door in Mr. Shouse's face.

Being a first-year administrator is difficult, but having to supervise the superintendent's wife would make this first year even more difficult. Mr. Shouse decided that he needed to brief Mr. Waned about the situation, and he hoped that the principal would give him some sound advice. However, he recalled his colleagues' advice and worried how it would look for a new AP to run to the principal for help. His future goals were to become a principal, but he was stuck in a hard place, because he worried that if it looked like he was battling Mrs. Albert, he might end his career early. However, he knew that a teacher should never abuse students. He thought about his first steps that he needed to take.

WHAT ELSE DO I NEED TO KNOW?

The following is a brief insight to the issues presented in the case study, with a brief literature review to help give context to those issues.

Educator Code of Ethics

Usually, when people earn the privilege of working as a teacher in a school, they receive a copy of the Educator Code of Ethics (ECOE) along with their teaching certificate. This code is sacred and essential for all educators when they are working with other individuals on a school campus. Furthermore, receiving the ECOE in conjunction with their teaching certificate reminds educators of vital aspects of interacting with both students and adults on a campus. Most ECOEs include sections on ethical teacher behavior toward the profession, colleagues, students, parents, and the community. Unfortunately, some educators do not behave ethically, either because it is a personal choice or because they do not believe that the code of ethics pertains to them.

Even more disturbing is that the ECOE is something that some in the profession do not even know exists. As Umpstead, Brady, Lugg, Klinker, and Thompson (2013) noted in their research, many educator preparation programs do not adequately cover the topic of ethics and professional responsibility, which may be a reason why some teachers face "...challenges ...in the classroom environment where they teach and guide the character development of our nation's youth" (p. 184). This revelation is a bit concerning, as the code of ethics usually parallels the values of the community and what the community at large expects to see ethically. "Codes of ethics are social instruments that reflect the morality of the day and the community" (p. 187). Hence, when a teacher is unaware of the ECOE, they may also be unaware of the expectations of morality a community holds sacred.

To ensure that educators are displaying ethical behavior, many states have codified an ECOE that focuses on guiding educators. As these states have a codified expectation of educator behavior, legal ramifications can occur when an educator ignores or refuses to follow an established ECOE. Some ramifications might simply be the sanctioning of a teacher certificate or, more severely, revocation of the certificate and termination from an educational position. This may be a main factor as to why so many current media stories focus on teacher misbehavior and unethical displays.

Hatcher and Storberg-Walker (2003) proposed that there are reasons to promote ethics, which mainly center on the expectations of a community and the local and state governments:

1 the public's expectation that educators act ethically;
2 the possibility of harm to learners;
3 the requirement to comply with applicable laws and regulations;
4 the protection of learners' well-being; and
5 the need to promote personal and community morality. (p. 22)

These reasons align with many codified ECOEs, which support that ethical behavior is a universal expectation and that it is "...a framework to guide ... educators and institutions through which they work in attaining the highest degree of professionalism" (Anonymous, 2005, p. 53).

Now, given our example of Mr. Shouse and Mrs. Albert, how does one educator work with another who disregards the ECOE and other campus and district policies? Are there any repercussions for educators who do not follow the ECOE, and can educators really lose their jobs if they disregard these ethics? And, when practice becomes an unwritten policy, such as "Don't mess with the superintendent's wife," can something be done to stop the practice? The short answer to each of these questions is yes. Many school districts wisely include the ECOE in educator employment contracts, written statements of policies and procedures, and teacher appraisals, all of which are related to whether educators may or may not retain their jobs. In other words, educators have indeed lost their jobs for violating the ECOE— and some have also lost their certification and even have been arrested— but when school districts take action against an educator for one incident or for recurring behavior, they usually do so because the educator has defied policies, codes, or laws that are mentioned in the ECOE.

Culture and Climate

For any educator working on any campus, knowledge of the school's culture and climate are extremely important, because the culture includes the shared beliefs, values, customs, and expectations of the campus community. These elements are essential to ensuring that all persons on a campus are healthy, engaged, and successful. For example, a campus may have a culture in which students and teachers are allowed to have tattoos and piercings showing, whereas, another campus may not allow anyone to have tattoos or piercings that are visible. Additionally, the climate of a school is its emotional atmosphere. For instance, when parents walk onto a campus, do they feel welcomed or do they feel like intruders? Do the students seem happy in their achievements, or are chaos and dysfunction apparent?

Here is a simple definition for culture and how an educator behaves: An educator helps shape the organization, and the organization shapes the educator. How much influence an educator has on an organization can be seen by the changes that are made per that individual educator's influence or presence. Goldman illustrated this definition when referring to leaders and the culture that they shape within an organization: "Leadership style reflects deeply held personal or organization values" (as cited in Kowalski, 2011, p. 64); and these deeply held personal or organizational values will dictate to those on a campus the worth that each person is given. In other words, the more worth given to an individual could mean the more shenanigans she will be able to get away with on a campus.

Another way to think of culture is through cultural proficiency. According to Lindsey, Robins, and Terrell (2009), "The cultural proficient leader is cognizant of her own culture, in its broadest definition; the culture of her school and district; and the cultures of her students and their families" (p. 127). This means that a leader understands how her cultural upbringing may affect things done on a campus and that the cultural upbringing of others may affect what they do on a campus. Understanding that there are different cultures that come together on a campus is to understand that there are different people that come together on a campus. Everyone is aware of everyone else's special contribution to the campus.

A final definition comes from Owens and Valesky (2011): Culture is defined as "...the characteristics of the total environment in a school building" (p. 137). They credit Renato and Tagiuri with describing the total environment of an organization, which includes the culture. Culture, then, is the "values, belief systems, norms, and whys of thinking that are characteristic of the people in the organization" often described as "the way we do things around here" (p. 138).

The many definitions of school climate mainly refer to the feeling one gets when walking through a school. Loukas (2007) found that a climate refers to the feelings and attitudes that are invoked by the environment of the school. School climate can also be referred to as "...setting the tone for all the learning and teaching done in the school environments and... it is predictive of students' ability to learn and develop in healthy ways" (National School Climate Center, 2014, para 1). Cohen (2011) defined school climate as referring to

> ...the quality and character of school life. School climate is based on patterns of students', parents', and school personnel's experience of school life and reflects norms, goals, values, interpersonal relationships, teaching and learning practices, and organizational structures. (p. 1)

These climate definitions show that like the culture, it is the people within an organization that set the climate of the school.

Numerous variables affect a school's culture and climate, such as the culture and climate of the school district and of the community. When the district's expectations favor certain individuals above others, dissension and disunity will result. Additionally, when some people do not have to follow the rules that others must obey, educators within the district may lose their motivation to do what is right. Hence, the culture and climate of a campus are greatly affected by those of the central office and the community. In the case of Mr. Shouse and Mrs. Albert, the perceptions and actions of the superintendent and the school board and their lack of support for the PVHS students, parents, and other educators are variables that influence the school in significant ways.

The climate and culture of a campus, a school district, and a community can also affect the job performance of an educator. When an educator becomes an AP, his/her political career has begun. An administrator must work tactfully with a variety of personality types and expectations, just as politicians do. Thus, to achieve effective and consistent job performance, a new AP must quickly learn how to politick while complying with all the applicable policies, procedures, expectations, codes, and laws. Additionally, being kind and supportive, yet firm, can help a new AP to eventually earn a school principalship based on merit.

When a new AP is assigned to a campus, the teachers, students, parents, and everyone else who works on that campus will be interested in how the newcomer fares on the job. Some persons may challenge the new AP or ingratiate themselves with him or her. Parents and others with some clout may inform the principal and the superintendent of their impressions of the AP, which sometimes can make or break the AP's chances of promotion, especially if enough of them complain to school board members or central office administrators.

Administrators can make their own way, however, by performing all assigned duties ethically and resolutely. The administrator must cultivate the ability to work with a diverse collection of educators, other staff, students, and parents and help them to collaborate and get along with one another. Additional areas in which an administrator must excel, which can be found on some administrative evaluations, encompass student achievement; parental involvement; community involvement and service; understanding and support of the curriculum; and instructional success of teachers in the classroom.

Similarly, teachers are also evaluated on their performance of assigned duties, such as teaching the curriculum, ensuring student safety, and encouraging students to succeed in their coursework. Teachers must demonstrate that they understand the state and school district curriculum by imparting realistic and transferable skills and knowledge in an engaging and motivating way. Additionally, teachers are expected to work with parents as partners in creating a school environment where students are free to be successful academically, socially, and emotionally. All of this contributes to the culture and climate of the school.

NCZ—NO CONSEQUENCE ZONE

Answer the questions below by applying what you know about this case and thinking about the steps you would take if you were faced with this situation or a similar one.

1 The ECOE is becoming more prominent in decisions to terminate educator contracts. Look at your state's ECOE and determine which ethics Mrs. Albert violated through her actions.

    a. According to your state's ECOE and your school district's policies, could Mrs. Albert be relieved of her duties and her contract terminated for her actions?

    b. Besides losing her job, could Mrs. Albert face any other consequences for her actions in your state?

2 The actions of individuals on a campus affect its culture and climate.

    a. How did Mrs. Albert's actions affect the culture and climate of PVHS?

    b. What can Mr. Shouse do to help neutralize the negative effects on the school's culture and climate?

3 New APs may find themselves stuck in a situation that could influence how others see their potential as a future principal. Such situations may even harm their relevance as an administrator.

    a. When addressing Mrs. Albert's actions and the need to protect students in her class, what are Mr. Shouse's choices for handling this situation?

    b. What outcome do you think will evolve from each choice?

    c. Think about the desired end result and work backward. What steps does Mr. Shouse need to complete before he reports to Mr. Waned, and what does he need to prepare himself to hear from Mr. Waned?

    d. After he speaks to Mr. Waned, what immediate steps could Mr. Shouse take?

4 Teacher contracts can be difficult to terminate, depending on state and federal laws and whether a teacher union is involved.

    a. Does your state have a law that outlines the steps for terminating the contract of a teacher who has clearly violated the ECOE or the district's policies and procedures?

    b. Is there a district policy or a contract clause that you abide by in your current position that could help both Mr. Shouse and Mr. Waned recommend termination of Mrs. Albert's contract?

5 Let's step back and look at the big picture.

    a. What are the social and political implications for Mr. Shouse if he supports Lauren?

    b. What are they if he supports Mrs. Albert?

    c. How might this same case study play out in your own community?

REFERENCES

Anonymous. (2005). The ACTE Code of Ethics. *Techniques*, 80(8), 53–54.

Cohen, J. (2011). Jonathan Cohen on school climate: Engaging the whole village, teaching the whole child. *The Challenge: A Publication of the Office of Safe and Drug-Free Schools*, 16(4), 1–2.

Hatcher, T., & Storberg-Walker, J. (2003). Developing ethical adult educators: A re-examination of the need for a code of ethics. *Adult Learning*, 14(2), 21–24.

Kowalski, T. (2011). *Case studies on educational administration* (6th ed.). New York: Allyn & Bacon Educational Leadership.

Lindsey, R. B., Robins, K. N., & Terrell, R. D. (2009). *Cultural proficiency: A manual for school leaders*. Thousand Oaks. CA: Corwin.

Loukas, A. (2007). What is school climate? High quality school climate is advantageous for all students and may be particularly beneficial for at-risk students. *Leadership Compass*, 5(1), 1–3.

National School Climate Center (2014, October). What is school climate. Retrieved October 15, 2014, from http://www.schoolclimate.org/climate/faq.php

Owens, R., & Valesky, T. (2011). *Organizational behavior in education: Leadership and school reform* (10th ed.). Upper Sadler River, NJ: Pearson Education Inc.

Umpstead, R., Brady, K., Lugg, E., Klinker, J., & Thompson, D. (2013). Educator ethics: A comparison of teacher professional responsibility laws in four states. *Journal of Law and Education*, 42(2), 183–225.

Chapter 2

The Teacher Is a Sexual Predator

The protection of students is a primary goal on a campus, yet confronting wrongdoing can be a difficult job for any educator. For some educators, ignoring a problem, ignoring parents' concerns, and ignoring the harm done to students may seem to be an easier response. When confrontation of a serious situation is bypassed, however, horrible consequences usually follow. If evidence emerges that a colleague is not protecting students from harm or is actually harming students, uncovering the truth and working with that colleague in the meantime can be an almost unbearable burden for educators. The following case involves a teacher who represents a grave danger to the children on an elementary campus.

MR. HARKER AND MRS. TANNER

It is the first day of school at Boltonville Elementary School and the first day of Mr. Harker's second year as a kindergarten teacher there. Hired at age twenty-two last year, Mr. Harker is one of the youngest teachers on the campus. He is amiable and considerate, traits that have made him an easy person to collaborate with and befriend.

The parents and the students also love Mr. Harker because he is fun, good-looking, and a male. Usually, teachers at the elementary level are females, and the only other male instructor at Bolton is the PE coach. So when Mr. Harker came aboard, everyone was pleased to have another male presence as a role model for the students.

The principal of Bolton Elementary is Mrs. Tanner, who has held that position for the past seven years. The teachers and other staff respect her, as do the students and their parents. Mrs. Tanner has spent most of her career at the elementary level, formerly teaching kindergarten and first, third, and fifth grades. After fifteen years of teaching, she became a curriculum instructional specialist for the district. She then served as an assistant principal at another elementary school for two years before coming to Bolton as principal.

For the previous school year, the open staff positions included one for a kindergarten teacher. Mrs. Tanner went through many applications, but none of the candidates seemed to fit her expectations. She was seeking someone who would be easy to mold into the kind of teacher she wanted on her campus: one who follows directives, loves children, and is a team player. Additionally, she wanted a teacher who would fit in with the existing family of educators at Bolton. When she finally came across Mr. Harker's application, Mrs. Tanner believed that she had found just the teacher she was looking for, with the bonus that he would be another male on the faculty. Mrs. Tanner believed that parents liked having a male presence in their children's lives, so Mr. Harker was a dream choice.

Something Is Just Not Right

The first concerns about Mr. Harker's teaching came to light in the first few weeks into his first year at Bolton. A parent, Mrs. Hill, e-mailed Mr. Harker, asking him to explain why her daughter, Cora, was not allowed to go to the bathroom when she needed to. Mr. Harker did not reply, so Cora's mother re-sent her initial e-mail to Mr. Harker and copied it to Mrs. Tanner. Mr. Harker still did not respond, but Mrs. Tanner did. Before e-mailing Mrs. Hill, however, the principal asked Mr. Harker about the bathroom issue. Mr. Harker stated that there was no issue and that he allowed all his students to visit the bathroom whenever they needed to. Hence, Mrs. Tanner sent Mrs. Hill the following e-mail:

Mrs. Hill,

I hope you are having a great day today. As you know, Bolton Elementary teachers always place students first, and Mr. Harker is no exception. I am confident that he does not keep children from using the bathroom, and I will ensure that this continues to be the case. Mr. Harker is a wonderful teacher, as you already know, and I am so happy your Cora is in his class. Please rest assured that Cora will be well taken care of.

Have a Bolton-terrific day!

Mrs. Tanner

Mrs. Tanner did not hear back from Mrs. Hill until three weeks later, when she received this e-mail, which was copied to Mr. Harker:

Dear Mrs. Tanner,

I appreciate your recent e-mail assuring me that Cora and all the other children in Mr. Harker's class are allowed to use the bathroom when they ask. I have continued to e-mail and call Mr. Harker, asking him not only to respond about the children's use of the bathroom, which he has not done, but also to address my concern about Cora coming home with makeup on her face and wearing lacy clothing that is not hers. As of today, I have had no response from Mr. Harker about either of my concerns. Cora explained that she was in the home center of Mr. Harker's classroom, playing house with two other children. She was the mother, and this meant she was allowed to wear makeup and the lacy clothes, according to the rules of the center. She also explained that Mr. Harker likes taking pictures of the students when they are playing in the home center.

I am concerned about what is happening in Mr. Harker's classroom. I would like to set up a conference with both you and Mr. Harker as soon as possible. I am available anytime this week. Please contact me with a date and time we can meet.

Thank you,

Mrs. Hill

Mrs. Tanner was not disturbed by this e-mail, because she knew that Mr. Harker was allowing kindergarten students to dress up like their parents, with the girls wearing makeup and frilly clothes to make the home center seem more authentic. When she spoke to Mr. Harker about the picture taking, he explained that he took photos for his bulletin board and his weekly class letter that he sent home to parents. Mrs. Tanner believed Mr. Harker and told him that she supported him. When they both met with Mrs. Hill, they were successful in calming her anxieties.

As Mr. Harker's first year continued, the parents of several other students in his class sent e-mails that focused on seemingly small issues about the home center, such as students coming home in makeup and different clothes and pictures being taken of the students. Some of these complaints, however, were about students not being able to use the bathroom, even though there was one within the classroom. Mrs. Tanner believed Mr. Harker every time he told her that the parents were exaggerating their concerns, and he even invited Mrs. Tanner and the parents into his classroom to see how healthy the environment was for the students. When Mrs. Tanner and the parents did visit the classroom, everything always seemed perfect, and the students were happily learning and using the bathroom at will.

During Mr. Harker's second year, parents lodged the same kinds of complaints almost daily in e-mails to him. Mr. Harker believed that the parents were not really that worried about their own kids but were just trying to get him fired, and he did not understand the drastic change from the previous year, when every parent and student wanted a chance to work in the "Harker Room." He felt betrayed, especially around the fourth week after the school year began, when parents started criticizing his "strange ways" and "weird ways of teaching." One parent sent this e-mail to both Mr. Harker and Mrs. Tanner:

Hello, Mr. Harker,

I am Kelley Martz's mother, and I would like to schedule a conference with you concerning my daughter's progress in your classroom. She started the year off loving going to school and being in your classroom. Only four weeks into the school year, Kelley now cries each morning on the way to school. When I ask her why she is crying, she just says she hates school. This is a concern for my husband and me, because why would a vivacious kindergartener hate school, especially when she was so eager to start school and liked it so much at first? Please let me know immediately when we can meet. My husband and I can meet whenever it is most convenient for you.

I am copying your principal on this message because I'd like her to meet with us too.

Sincerely,

Mrs. Martz

Mrs. Martz never met with Mr. Harker, but she did meet with Mrs. Tanner. The principal said that she had performed several walk-thrus of Mr. Harker's classroom and that it was always one of the highest-performing and best-run rooms on campus. After reassuring Mrs. Martz, Mrs. Tanner took her to observe Mr. Harker's classroom. Although Mrs. Martz still felt concerned, she left the school without any further discussion.

A week later, another parent sent a handwritten note to Mr. Harker by placing it inside her son's backpack. The note read:

Mr. Harker,

Call me ASAP and let me know when I can meet with you about my son Trevor. He has told me that you are taking pictures of him while he is in the bathroom and that you make him play in the home center when he would rather play in the construction center. I am very upset and want a meeting ASAP, BECAUSE YOU NEED TO STOP TAKING PICTURES OF MY SON WITHOUT MY PERMISSION!!! I will come in today to speak with you.

Ms. Miller

Ms. Miller showed up at lunchtime to eat with Trevor and signed in at the front office. Before walking to the lunchroom, she asked to speak with Mr. Harker. The office secretary told her that Mr. Harker was on his duty-free lunchtime and that she would need to make an appointment with him. Upon hearing this, Ms. Miller became enraged, and the secretary called Mrs. Tanner to the office. Ms. Miller explained her concern to the principal, who tried to calm the mother by telling her what a wonderful addition Mr. Harker was to the campus. Mrs. Tanner then asked Mr. Harker to come to her office to speak with Ms. Miller. When he arrived, Mr. Harker immediately apologized for being too busy to respond to e-mails and for the miscommunications that her son was passing on to her, adding that he would be available to Ms. Miller at any time and inviting her to become a class mom. Ms. Miller was not appeased and demanded that she be allowed to observe her son's room immediately and to have her concerns addressed. She also stated that if she had to, she would go to the superintendent and then the media. "I will not be ignored," she insisted.

Mrs. Tanner told the worried mother that Mr. Harker had in fact addressed her concerns and that bullying tactics would not work at Bolton Elementary. Furthermore, Mrs. Tanner explicitly supported Mr. Harker and his instructional methods, because he was a great male influence and role model. She then gave Ms. Miller the superintendent's phone number and said, "It's your right to call our superintendent, if that's what you want to do. But we are serious about our students here at Bolton, and I cannot sit here any longer as you slander Mr. Harker." At this, Ms. Miller calmly retorted, "It is a sad day when students are not given the same devotion that you have so blindly shown for Mr. Harker." Then she walked out of Mrs. Tanner's office and drove straight to central office to complain to the superintendent.

By the time the Christmas holidays were approaching, more and more parents complained to Mrs. Tanner about Mr. Harker. They asked her to stop patronizing them and to instead investigate their growing concerns that something just was not right in Mr. Harker's class. One parent who did not want Mrs. Tanner to waste any more time went directly to the superintendent, Dr. Kyle, to let her know about the parents' concerns and to inform her that he would report Mr. Harker to the police if she did not act quickly.

What Next?

By the beginning of the second semester, Superintendent Kyle had received five phone calls and three visits from different parents, complaining that Mr. Harker was scaring their children, not teaching them. The parents also were unhappy that Mrs. Tanner enabled Mr. Harker to do whatever he wanted in his classroom and that she disregarded their concerns, refusing to take seriously any complaint that contradicted her belief that Mr. Harker was a fantastic teacher. The parents were baffled, because they remembered in previous situations that Mrs. Tanner had always demanded evidence from them when she followed up on a complaint, and they expected her to do the same now. They wanted to see evidence to confirm or disconfirm what their children were telling them. Instead, Mrs. Tanner was giving them only empty words.

One parent relayed to Dr. Kyle an example of Mrs. Tanner's insistence in the past that evidence be provided to support a parent's complaint. The example involved a boy and his fourth-grade teacher, who accused the boy of stealing pencils and candy from the class treasure box. The teacher contacted both the parent and Mrs. Tanner about the theft. Mrs. Tanner asked the teacher for proof of the theft and for the names of any witnesses and then gave both the teacher and the student opportunities to tell their side of the story. After gathering all the available data, Mrs. Tanner decided to give the fourth grader a three-day in-school suspension and to require that he replace all the stolen items. Although the boy's dad was upset about the situation, he had respected Mrs. Tanner for treating his son fairly.

Now, however, the parents' complaints were too numerous for Dr. Kyle to ignore. She met with Mrs. Tanner and instructed her to talk to Mr. Harker about the complaints and determine whether there was any truth to them. She also directed Mrs. Tanner to maintain detailed documentation of her communications with parents, Mr. Harker, students, and any other persons who had insight regarding the complaints. Finally, Dr. Kyle told Mrs. Tanner that given what the parents were alleging and the panic she heard in their voices, a lawsuit might be on the horizon, and that would not be good for the district.

Later, and after Mrs. Tanner had spoken with all concerned, she met with Dr. Kyle. Her documentation included grave evidence supporting the parents' allegations. In Mr. Harker's desk she had found photographs of students in questionable positions, and she eventually learned why his students were not always allowed to use the restroom. When a student needed to use the bathroom, Mr. Harker would go into the room with the student, and when he was not available, he made students wait until he could go with them. Mrs. Tanner also informed Dr. Kyle of other shocking information she had uncovered about the teacher's behaviors that seemed abusive, such as making them wear cloth diapers, which he made, with plastic underwear to go over the cloth diaper instead of going in the toilet and making them totally undress to put on costumes when playing in the centers. Therefore, Dr. Kyle contacted the school district lawyer and the school board president and explained to them that the next calls she would make would be to Child Protective Services and the local police department.

The ensuing police investigation found that Mr. Harker had taken photographs of the children in his kindergarten class since he started at Bolton Elementary. Some of these pictures showed the children naked, on the toilet, and in suggestive poses. Mr. Harker was arrested, and investigators found child pornography on both his school and home computers and elsewhere in his apartment. The school community was distraught, and Mrs. Tanner weighed her options on what was best for her—and retirement looked really good. The parents? They were beyond angry and contacted the local newspaper and asked for their story to be printed on Sunday. They also met with a lawyer to prepare a lawsuit against the school district, Dr. Bale, Mrs. Tanner, and Mr. Harker.

WHAT ELSE DO I NEED TO KNOW?

The following is a brief insight to the issues presented in the case study, with a brief literature review to help give context to those issues.

Protecting Students from Pedophiles

How can educators learn to recognize a pedophile, especially one who hides behind a facade of friendliness and caring? What responsibilities do a school principal and other educators have if they or parents suspect that a campus staff member may be a pedophile? And if that person is in fact found to be a pedophile, where does accountability for the situation lie, and what responsibilities do a school principal and other educators have?

So, what is pedophilia, and is it the same as a child molester? In a research study done by Sartorius et al. (2008), it was concluded that

> As pedophilia is characterized by socially deviant, repetitive, highly arousing sexual fantasies, urges and activities, it shares some phenomenological similarities with obsessive-compulsive disorders (OCDs), which are also characterized by inadequate urges and poorly inhibited, repetitive behavior. (p. 275)

This definition gives some insight into the characteristics of a pedophile, but some believe that there is a distinction between a pedophile and a child molester.

Feelgood and Hoyer (2008) defined a child molester as "a person who has had sexual contact with children...The term 'child molester' reflects behaviours, specifications of which vary among justice systems and across time" (p. 34). The term *pedophile*, according to the American Psychiatric Association (APA) and the World Health Organization, "applies to people who have a sexual interest (or even preference) in pre-pubescent children independent of their actual behaviours, legal or otherwise" (as cited in Feelgood & Hoyer, 2008, p. 34). And, in an article by Murray (2000), pedophiles and child molesters are mostly male, can be heterosexual, homosexual, or bisexual, and may prefer adult sex partners but target children due to their availability and vulnerability. Additionally, the perpetrator is usually sixteen years old or older, their victims are usually five years of age or older and, most times, pedophiles are relatives, friends, or neighbors (Murray, 2000).

In Finkelhor's (2009) research, it was found that most pedophiles, or sexual abusers, were not strangers and that about a third were juveniles, or minors, themselves. Additionally, Finkelhor defined child molesters, sexual abusers, and child sex offenders as "including the entire spectrum of sexual crimes and offenses in which children up to age seventeen are victims" (pp. 170–171). It was also established in his article that the stereotype of a sex abuser is not fully correct. Most pedophiles are never caught, arrested, or convicted, and about half of those who have been caught are post-pubescent, ranging in age from twelve to seventeen, which would mean that they could not qualify as pedophiles (p. 172). Further, about half of child abuse cases involve young offender, or juveniles, who choose victims younger than thirteen, which means that they, too, do not qualify as pedophiles.

Then, there are those who believe a workable definition has not been established. As McCartan (2011) explained

> Understanding and responding to paedophiha is a multi-disciplinary... multi-agency endeavour, with a broad gamut of different professions and a variety of different professionals involved, ...those involved in the treatment of paedophiles (therapists/clinical practitioners); those who investigate, prosecute, punish and monitor paedophiles (criminal justice practitioners). (p. 333)

McCartan further asserted that a more realistic and empirically based definition that is non-academic and easy to understand is what is needed when defining what pedophilia is or is not.

Due to the different interpretations of who is or is not a pedophile, child molester, or child sex offender, it is best to refer to your state codes. For the purpose of the rest of this chapter, pedophile and child abuser will be used interchangeably.

From the start, educators should learn about the known characteristics and behaviors of pedophiles, child molesters, or child sex offenders by reading literature on the subject. One good place to start is with your state's penal or criminal code, specifically sexual assault or abuse of a minor. The code will help you understand what the law states and will give you a better understanding of how you may proceed if a pedophile is on your campus. Some examples of what the code may show can be seen in the Tennessee Code Annotated and the Wyoming Statute. Sexual assault with a minor is defined in the Tennessee Code Annotated, Title 39 Criminal Offenses, Chapter 13 Offenses Against Person, Part 5 Sexual Offenses as

Sexual contact with a minor—Sexual contact by an authority figure.

(a) It is an offense for a defendant to engage in unlawful sexual contact with a minor when:

(1) The minor is at least thirteen (13) but less than eighteen (18) years of age;

(2) The defendant is at least four (4) years older than the victim; and

(3) The defendant was, at the time of the offense, in a position of trust, or had supervisory or disciplinary power over the minor by virtue of the defendant's legal, professional, or occupational status and used the position of trust or power to accomplish the sexual contact; or

(4) The defendant had, at the time of the offense, parental or custodial authority over the minor and used the authority to accomplish the sexual contact.

(b) As used in this section, "sexual contact" means the defendant intentionally touches or kisses the minor's lips with the defendant's lips if such touching can be reasonably construed as being for the purpose of sexual arousal or gratification.

(c) Sexual contact by an authority figure is a Class A misdemeanor with a mandatory minimum fine of one thousand dollars ($1,000).

(d) Each instance of unlawful sexual contact shall be considered a separate offense.

In Wyoming, sexual abuse with a minor is defined in Title 6 Crimes and Offenses, Chapter 2 Offenses Against the Person, Article 3 Sexual Assault as

Sexual abuse of a minor in the first degree; penalties.

(a) An actor commits the crime of sexual abuse of a minor in the first degree if:

(i) Being sixteen (16) years of age or older, the actor inflicts sexual intrusion on a victim who is less than thirteen (13) years of age;

(ii) Being eighteen (18) years of age or older, the actor inflicts sexual intrusion on a victim who is less than eighteen (18) years of age, and the actor is the victim's legal guardian or an individual specified in W.S. 6-4-402;

(iii) Being eighteen (18) years of age or older, the actor inflicts sexual intrusion on a victim who is less than sixteen (16) years of age and the actor occupies a position of authority in relation to the victim.

(b) Except as provided in subsection (c) of this section, a person convicted under subsection (a) of this section is subject to imprisonment for not more than fifty (50) years, unless the person convicted qualifies under W.S. 6-2-306(e).

(c) A person convicted under paragraph (a)(i) of this section, where the actor is at least twenty-one (21) years of age, is subject to imprisonment for not less than twenty-five (25) years nor more than fifty (50) years, unless the person convicted qualified under W.S. 6-2-306(e).

As can be seen, the age of the minor will be different from state to state, and the specifics of what constitutes sexual assault or abuse of a minor will be specified in the code or statutes. Again, educators should understand this part of the law to understand what constitutes a sexual abuse of a minor in a state.

Unfortunately, with the news stories that seem prolific concerning teachers having sexual affairs or contact with students, there have also been many court cases that have involved the sexual assault or harassment of a student by a teacher or other educator. Educators who understand what these court cases assert will have a better understanding of what their role must be when working with students and teachers on a campus. For instance, in *Franklin v. Gwinnett County Public Schools* (1992), Fossey and DeMitchell established that the case, which involved sexual harassment between a student and teacher, did not give a clear framework for educators in understanding their responsibility to provide an atmosphere free from harassment (as cited in Spain, 2010, p. 7). However, in *Gebser v. Lago Vistas Independent School District* (1998), it was determined that educators who knew of a sexual misconduct or harassment of a student and did not act would be liable for monetary damages under Title IX. Furthermore, Walsh, Kemerer, and Maniotis emphasized that in *Doe v Taylor I.S.D.* (1994), a student has a constitutional right to be free of any type of sexual abuse, which the Fifth Circuit ruled in answering the questions "which included a student's right to be free of sexual abuse at school, to be protected by the U.S. Constitution, and to make school employees accountable for protection of the student" (as cited in Spain, 2010, p. 8). These cases illuminate the duty of educators to do whatever possible to ensure students are protected from any person who may exhibit sexual misconduct or harassment.

Administrators and other educators must not dismiss any reports of harm to another person on a campus. Ignoring such reports, regardless of whether they are true or are not, can only hurt the persons involved, including administrators who choose to do nothing about a tip and then find themselves without a job—or worse. An administrator must take seriously any report of a possible criminal act, including sexual abuse and pedophilia. However, there have been instances when a student or group of students accused a teacher of sexual abuse and then later admitted they were lying. False accusations of pedophilia can destroy an individual's career and personal life, even if the accused is officially cleared of all charges. Hence, administrators must be cautious and should remind all campus personnel to stay clear of any and all situations that could be perceived as inappropriate behavior with a student.

When it comes to hiring of personnel, despite the best efforts of administrators, a pedophile sometimes gets hired. Typically, a pedophile will endeavor to develop positive relationships with coworkers and supervisors, counting on people's tendency to give friends and acquaintances the benefit of the doubt when bizarre accusations are made or indicators of inappropriate conduct are present. Your acceptance of the fact that you cannot know another person completely, along with your knowledge of the common characteristics of pedophiles, will serve you well if you are ever confronted by a case such as Mr. Harker's.

In particular, administrators who are responsible for hiring teachers and other campus staff should have a basic knowledge of pedophilia and an awareness that pedophiles often seek jobs that involve frequent contact with children. If not qualified for a professional position, pedophiles may attempt to acquire volunteer work with children, often in a supervisory capacity, such as substitute teaching, sports coaching, or tutoring, or in some other position that involves unsupervised time with children. During job interviews, pedophiles often will refer to children in idealistic terms, such as "pure," "heavenly," and "innocent" and may be over-insistent that the "children are the future." Follow your instincts if an applicant's descriptions of children are inappropriate and exaggerated, and do not allow the person on your campus in either a paid or unpaid position. Also remember that although pedophiles are much more likely to be males than females, some are indeed females.

Due Process with Teachers

When you must deal with situations in which allegations have been made about a teacher, a student, or any other person on your campus, gathering as much information as possible from those involved is required and will help you to make a professional, data-driven decision. This gathering of data and documentation is a part of giving "due process" to the alleged wrongdoer and demonstrates that you have acted in good faith in attempting to prove or disprove an allegation. Simply put, due process is the proper and legal way of allowing all parties in a situation to tell their side of the story and explain their understanding of what occurred and allowing those who have been accused to defend themselves against any allegations. This process enables you to gather written and verbal statements from each person and then, after reviewing all the information, to make a professional judgment about what to do next.

When you are presented with an accusation of any kind about someone on your campus, especially one that might lead to an arrest, we suggest that you take the following steps:

1 Obtain a statement from the accuser. When a person is accusing another of wrongdoing, ask the accuser to start at the beginning and describe the details of what has occurred. After telling you verbally about the problem, either the accuser can write down the details or you can write them down as the accuser relates them to you. Then read the statement aloud so that both of you can hear what is on paper, allow the accuser to make any necessary corrections or additions, and have the accuser sign and date the statement.

2 Inform the accused, obtain statements from all other parties involved, and take appropriate action. After an allegation has been made, inform the accused person about it, and give that person a chance to tell his/her side of the story both verbally and in writing. If the allegation is something that is manageable at the campus level and you will be the main person handling the situation, also allow each of the other relevant parties to voice his or her side of the story. Afterward, make a professional judgment about what to do next.

If the allegation is one that may involve a penal code violation, however, as soon as the allegation is made, you should immediately contact your superiors, according to the district's chain of command (e.g., principal, assistant superintendent, and/or human resources manager), and contact your school resource officer or community police officer. When you contact them, let them know what the allegation is, what steps you have performed already, what steps you will take to gather more information, and when and how you will keep them apprised of new developments. After you have investigated thoroughly, including obtaining statements from all involved, make a recommendation to your supervisors, such as a leave of absence or a contract termination for the accused. Be careful, however, and be sure that you have enough information before contacting your bosses and the police, especially when it comes to an accusation that could lead to an arrest. For example, if you are hearing for the first time that a teacher is having a sexual relationship with a student, you should tell the teacher about the allegation and give him or her a chance to refute or confirm the allegation. You should also observe the teacher and the student together. If no real evidence can point to anything improper, remind the teacher to refrain from any behaviors that could be misconstrued. Conversely, if you have heard the same accusation more than once from different persons, contacting your supervisors and police would be prudent and warranted.

3 Contact the parents. One of the hardest things you may have to do is to contact parents to tell them that their child was harmed at your school. In incidents involving penal code violations, the school district lawyer may be contacted, and the lawyer will counsel you on how to proceed and what to say to the parents. In some cases, the lawyer or the superintendent will be the one who contacts the parents.

4 Make a data-based decision. After you have collected all the data necessary for reaching a professional decision, carry out a reprimand or a warning to the accused teacher, place notes about the incident in the teacher's personnel file for inclusion in his or her evaluation, or apply whatever other type of consequence is appropriate.

In any situation involving an allegation against a teacher or other staff member, be direct and honest with the accused person so that there is no room for misinterpretation of what you mean. You must be sure to use the language of the school board–approved policies; doing so will help you if must later appear in court. If a teacher is accused of hitting a student, for example, tell him or her that if the allegation proves to be true, the teacher's contract will be terminated and that if the police develop probable cause, the teacher will also be arrested for assault.

Document everything! In all that you do, especially if you have to make professional judgment calls as an administrator, document every single step you take toward the resolution of a situation. In many states, an education or government code or law describes the steps an administrator must take to resolve or address a wrongdoing. This code or law typically includes a "good faith" clause that protects administrators who have followed the law and have done everything in their power to resolve and right a situation. No matter what the crisis, do something that will help to prevent harm to another person on your campus: Ask questions, find supporting evidence, consult your superiors. Do not make the mistake of taking no action.

NCZ—NO CONSEQUENCE ZONE

Answer the questions below by applying what you know about this case and thinking about the steps you would take if you were faced with this situation or a similar one.

1 Parents always have concerns about their children. Most of the concerns they express to you will be relatively easy to address. However, some concerns, such as those presented in this case, can be hard to hear and accept. Especially at such times, you must maintain

your objectivity and base your decisions on facts, *not* on emotions or relationships.

   a. If you were the principal of Bolton Elementary, what would you have done differently after the first parent expressed her concern to you about what was happening in Mr. Harker's classroom?

   b. What steps can you take when listening to a complaint from a parent?

   c. After hearing some complaints about Mr. Harker during his first year at Bolton, how would you have responded to parents who voiced similar concerns during his second year?

2 Identifying sexual predators is a necessary task for an administrator. Sometimes, though, it might not seem plausible that a teacher who has gone through a background check and the fingerprint process would be classified as a sexual predator.

   a. What procedures are in place within your school district that may help you identify sexual predators?

   b. What are your district's policies for recommending termination of a teacher's contract once he or she has been identified as a sexual predator?

   c. What does your state penal code say about sex offenders, especially on a school campus?

   d. What does your state's education code say?

3 Safety policies and procedures are essential when working with children and other adults on a campus. Performing background checks and fingerprinting on all prospective staff members and volunteers is an excellent way to find out whether they should be allowed near children.

   a. Do your district's policies for hiring staff and volunteers include background checks and fingerprinting? Are any other procedures and policies in place for vetting new personnel?

   b. What are the requirements for a parent or other family member to be accepted as a volunteer at your school?

4 When parents feel trapped or helpless, they may threaten to "have your job," "talk to your boss," or "report you to the authorities."

   a. How would you have responded to the parents in this case who threatened to take their complaints to the superintendent and the media?

   b. What are some techniques you can use to remain calm and objective when interacting with an upset parent?

5 Now let us look at the big picture surrounding this case.

   a. What are the social, political, and educational implications of Mrs. Tanner's avoidance of confronting and thereby preventing Mr. Harker's ongoing pedophilia?

b. What are the social, political, and educational implications of this incident for the community?

REFERENCES

Feelgood, S., & Hoyer, J. (2008). Child molester or paedophile? Sociolegal versus psychopathological classification of sexual offenders against children. *Journal of Sexual Aggression*, 14(1), 33–43.

Finkelhor, D. (2009). The prevention of childhood sexual abuse. *The Future of Children*, 19(2), 169–194.

McCartan, K. (2011). Professional responses to contemporary discourses and definitions of paedophilia. *International Journal of Police Science & Management*, 13(4), 322–335.

Murray, J. (2000). Psychological profile of pedophiles and child molesters. *The Journal of Psychology*, 134(2), 211–224.

Sartorius, A., Ruf, M., Kief, C., Demirakca, T., Bailer, J., Ende, G., Henn, F., Meyer-Lindenberg, A., & Dressing, H. (2008). Abnormal amygdala activation profile in pedophilia. *European Archives of Psychiatry & Clinical Neuroscience*, 258, 271–277, DOI:10.1007/s00406-008-0782-2

Spain, C. (2010). *Practices and policies in high schools to prevent educator-to-student sexual misconduct: A principal's study of knowledge and experiences* (Doctoral dissertation). University of North Texas, ProQuest, UMI Dissertations Publishing.

Tennessee Code Annotated § 39-13-509 (2014)

Wyoming Statute § 6-2-314 (2014)

Chapter 3

The Online Lies That Grew and Grew

An old adage advises that if you do not have anything nice to say, you should not say anything at all. In today's social media universe, however—where some consider etiquette, tact, and self-restraint to be irrelevant—such a suggestion might be viewed as quaint. Furthermore, social media have become an easy avenue for troublemakers, often cloaked by anonymity, to skewer others by making malicious accusations without offering evidence to support them. In the following case, an incoming high school principal new to the district is blindsided by spiteful, unfounded rumors posted about her online as she tries to settle into her administrative role. Although the protagonist in this case study is a principal, any educator at any level could potentially face a similar situation.

THE CASE

The Championship-Coach-Turned-Principal

Aqua Springs High School (ASHS) in a suburb of the city of Springstone Bluff was built in 2007 and opened in 2008 to accommodate the school district's growing student population. Its first principal was Coach Monnett, a beloved coach who had served for twenty-one years at the district's Lonesome Lake High School before going straight to his first principalship, at ASHS. He was renowned locally for leading Lonesome Lake's football team, the Lions, to three regional and four state championships during his last seven years there, and when the district's board redrew school boundaries to include the new high school, many of the students and families he had known at Lonesome Lake High were shifted to ASHS's jurisdiction. Because of his lengthy winning streak with the Lions, the entire city was happy to see the revered coach promoted to ASHS principal, even though he had no prior experience as an administrator. It turned out that his leadership style was so laissez-faire that it was almost nonexistent, but his many supporters tended to overlook his administrative shortcomings.

For four years, Coach Monnett led ASHS by delegating all his duties and spending most days at the local coffee shop, visiting with parents and other community members. At times, one could find "Coach" on the golf course with city council members who were lifelong friends of his, talking about the good old days or upcoming family events. Whenever issues arose at ASHS, the assistant principals (APs) and secretaries handled them and eventually were seen as the school's true leaders. Although no major problems occurred under Coach's leadership, ASHS was becoming known as a school where "the inmates were running the asylum," because it did not have a "real" principal.

During the summer before Coach Monnett's fifth year as principal, the district superintendent retired, and a new superintendent, Dr. Hiram Gregory, was hired. The school board charged Dr. Gregory with reviewing the principal at each campus and making recommendations about contract renewals and non-renewals for the following year. Although the board members did not give Dr. Gregory a reason for performing this particular task, they stressed that some campuses were not as successful as they had hoped.

Within the first few months of observing the administration at ASHS in Coach Monnett's fifth year as a principal, Dr. Gregory clearly understood the school board's concerns about principal contracts, even though the board had not specifically mentioned Coach Monnett. Dr. Gregory had visited each campus in the district twice within the first three months of the school year, and each time he visited ASHS, Coach Monnett was not available. Both times, his secretary told Dr. Gregory that the principal was in meetings. During his third visit in late January to ASHS, Dr. Gregory asked whether Coach was on campus, and when the secretary again replied that he was in a meeting, the superintendent told her to call him and tell him to get to the campus ASAP. Within twenty minutes, Coach was in his office with Dr. Gregory.

Through this impromptu meeting, it became obvious to Dr. Gregory that Coach Monnett was unfamiliar with the curriculum that was being taught at ASHS, what the Student Code of Conduct stated about suspensions and expulsions, or which state assessments the students would take throughout the year. Additionally, when Dr. Gregory asked Coach which teachers on his campus could be classified as master, skilled, and unskilled, the principal could not answer. After the meeting, Coach Monnett was given notice that his contract would not be renewed for the upcoming year. As his contract was up for renewal that year anyway, no settlement or breaking of his contract would occur, and he decided to simply retire.

The New ASHS Principal

Mrs. Sally Tacumah started her education career in a suburb of a large city seventeen years ago. She taught tenth-grade advanced placement world history for four years and eleventh-grade advanced placement United States history for seven years. Recognized as a strong and masterful teacher, she was promoted to assistant principal at the same high school, and she was quite successful and well respected during her six years in that position. Last June she decided to take a principalship in the suburb of Aqua Springs, where a friend and former colleague of hers, Dr. Gregory, was now superintendent.

After the decision was made not to renew Coach Monnett's contract as principal of ASHS, Superintendent Gregory knew instantly whom he wanted to lead the school: Sally Tacumah. As her superior during her time as a teacher and an AP, he had always had high hopes for her, and he knew she could help the students and teachers of ASHS to be successful in the upcoming school year. He also knew, however, that some parents and city council members believed that Coach Monnett—"the greatest coach," in their opinion—was being mistreated by not having his principal's contract renewed, and around the city, sentiments toward himself as superintendent had become divisive. He hoped that the animosity some people felt toward him would not affect Mrs. Tacumah or ASHS.

Mrs. Tacumah was looking forward to starting her principalship under Dr. Gregory's leadership, and she wanted to get to know the teachers before ASHS started its sixth year in existence. While collaborating with the school's teachers over the summer, she had found many areas that needed attention, such as the curriculum, student performance, assessments, and teacher evaluations. She hoped that with the staff, students, parents, and community members working together, ASHS would be transformed in beneficial ways. Many teachers had told her that they were ready for a change at ASHS, and after she began serving as principal, numerous people throughout the community praised her efforts.

Not everyone, however, thought that Mrs. Tacumah was a good thing for ASHS. In fact, people she did not even know were making defamatory statements about her, especially through a blog on the city newspaper's website. Although the blog posts about her focused on positive aspects of her new position, some community members attacked her from the beginning in comments on the blog, as the following examples show.

SpringstoneTribune.com
School Talk

New Principal at Aqua Springs HS: Sally Tacumah
Posted by the Tribune Newshound on August 13
The school year is about to start, and a new principal will be at the helm of Aqua Springs High School, since Coach Monnett retired last year. I'm told that the staff of ASHS are eager to welcome Sally Tacumah as their new administrator. She comes to ASHS with a background as a classroom teacher and an assistant principal and is likely to bring a new leadership style to the campus. Good luck, Mrs. Tacumah!

Comments
Posted by GR8123
School hasn't even started and already I miss Coach Monnett. I don't know this new principal, but I heard she has only been a teacher for 4 years and hasn't really been an assistant principal. WHY IS SHE THE PRINCIPAL OF AQUA SPRINGS HIGH SCHOOL?? AND WHAT'S UP WITH HER LAST NAME? IS SHE AN INDIAN?

Posted by silly mood
I heard that Sally is on her third marriage. What a loser!

Posted by Batboy12
I think she's been a teacher longer than 4 years, because she looks really old. I bet she won't be able to handle ASHS. I think she's an American Indian.

The second blog:

SpringstoneTribune.com
School Talk

Aqua Springs HS Is Off to a Good Start
Posted by the Tribune Newshound on September 20
It is Dr. Gregory's second year as Springstone Bluff's superintendent of schools, and he has already made some good decisions that have boosted student performance in the district. His most recent good decision was the appointment of Sally Tacumah as the principal of Aqua Springs High School. She seems to be well liked already—the teachers and students affectionately call her "Mrs. T." This school year promises to be a good one, and these good vibes are due to the decisions made by our superintendent and elected school board. Next time you see one of these folks, give him or her a high-five.

Comments
Posted by silly mood
Just got off the phone with a reliable source who told me that the new superintendent and the new ASHS principal are having an affair, and that's

how she got the job! Aaarrrggghhhhhh!!! The school board obviously didn't know this when they brought Dr. Gregory in.

Posted by 2hazy2day
All I need to know is: what will she do at ASHS that Coach Monnett hasn't? She can't live up to all that he has done for this city and this school district. We are all with you, Coach! #hatetacumah

The third blog:

SpringstoneTribune.com
School Talk

Is Mrs. T the Right Fit for Aqua Springs HS?
Posted by the Tribune Newshound on October 27
Not everyone loves Mrs. T after all. It is understandable that when an esteemed coach retires and is replaced with an "outsider," some parents might not be very happy about it. But when the outsider has proven to be genuine in how she conducts school business, the least we can do is give her a chance. Dr. Gregory and the board of trustees knew what they were doing when they hired Mrs. T, so let's give her time to implement her plans for ASHS. Many teachers, students, and parents feel that she has already demonstrated that she is capable and dedicated.

Comments
Posted by GR8123
How can you give someone a chance when she doesn't give my own kids a chance!? My kids came home and said they hate Mrs. Tacumah. They said she is an idiot. #hatetacumah #standupforourkids #coachmonnettrocks

Posted by EATBeef
Come on. We all need to give Mrs. Tacumah the same chance we gave Coach Monnett when he started as principal. She seems to be someone who can help our kids and teachers do better. Let's give her some time before we judge her.

Posted by Batboy12
Hey, EATBeef, you obviously didn't grow up here, so you don't know what this community needs—and we don't need Sally Tacumah here. She is an OUTSIDER! Next time, just keep your thoughts to yourself. #outsidergohome

Posted by EATBeef
It's a sad day when people try to censor those who don't agree with them. I hope only the best for this community, our children, and Mrs. Tacumah.

Posted by Batboy12
You're not listening, EATBeef! Go back to where you came from! OUTSIDER! #outsidergohome #hatetacumah

Mrs. T wasn't sure where the disdain expressed in the blog comments was coming from, and she felt helpless in controlling the attacks, because most were made online rather than face-to-face. Although she felt certain that she had the support of the majority of teachers, students, and parents, the barrage of lies and unfounded gossip was beginning to weigh on her. After she had been on the job only a couple of months, another disturbing development was announced on the *School Talk* blog.

The fourth blog:

SpringstoneTribune.com
School Talk

Petition Started to Oust Principal Sally Tacumah
Posted by the Tribune Newshound on November 15
Some community members have sent letters to the editor of the *Tribune,* claiming that they have started a petition to remove Sally Tacumah as the principal of Aqua Springs High. The *Tribune* has also received unconfirmed reports that one city council member is ready to sign the petition. A question that must be asked is, What has Mrs. T done to displease the creators of this petition?

A band of parents and teachers who support Mrs. T is also organizing. They believe that she is the best thing that has happened to ASHS in years, and they are prepared to start their own petition to keep Mrs. T on as their principal. We'll keep you posted on breaking news about this saga at ASHS.

Comments
Posted by silly mood
Just heard that "some" city council members (not just one) are petitioning to get rid of Mrs. Tacumah. Yes! #supportourkids #ridtacumah #staystrong

The fifth blog:

SpringstoneTribune.com
School Talk

Support for Sally Tacumah at Aqua Springs HS
Posted by the Tribune Newshound on December 2
What should have been the start of a good school year for a new principal and her staff and students has been sidetracked by a witch hunt based on nothing but hearsay. Although this witch hunt seems to have fizzled, some disgruntled parents still want Mrs. T removed from the ASHS principalship. One must ask whether the real reason for all of this uproar is that some people truly believe that Mrs. T isn't a good principal, or is it that Coach Monnett had to leave ASHS because his lack of leadership was detrimental to ASHS? Has any actual evidence been uncovered that points to the need to fire Mrs. T?

Comments

Posted by silly mood

Look, the evidence is in the way Mrs. T carries herself. I can plainly see that Mrs. T is self-absorbed and uncaring. She took this principal's position because she had nowhere else to go. And she took it knowing that our favorite coach was being forced to retire. What did she think would happen? AND what is detrimental to ASHS is this woman who just needs to go! #firetacumah

Posted by LooseLips

It has been more than two weeks since silly mood said that a petition was going around to remove Mrs. Tacumah and that city council members were going to sign it. I haven't seen it, but I want to sign it. I don't know Mrs. Tacumah, because my kids are in elementary school, but I am convinced that she needs to go, based on the comments on this blog and the unflattering rumors I have heard. My children deserve a better principal. Bring Coach Monnett back!!! #firetacumah #supportourkids

Posted by silly mood

Hey, everyone—great news! The next school board meeting will be on December 11, and we need as many people to come and rally against Sally Tacumah. And bring signs with you to show that we want to get rid of her! #firetacumah #outsidergohome #hatetacumah

Posted by EATBeef

Can someone please explain why Mrs. Tacumah is being petitioned against? I have two kids at ASHS and they love her. From what I have heard from teachers and other parents, she is already changing ASHS into a school that everyone wants to be a part of. She has been praised as the first REAL principal of ASHS, because she stays on campus and is very accessible. She meets and greets everyone who comes on campus.

Posted by 2hazy2day

Look, EATBeef. It is simple to understand. We all grew up with Coach Monnett and respect his coaching and leadership skills, especially since he took our football team to state four years in a row. He should have been allowed to stay at ASHS until he really wanted to retire. He had enough assistant principals and secretaries taking care of things when he wasn't around, and the school was just fine. Then the new superintendent goes and replaces this great man with a woman? Do you understand now? #bringbackmonnett #firetacumah

Posted by Batboy12

I'll be there, silly mood! We already have 5 signs made! EATBeef, nobody cares what you think, so just shut up! #outsidergohome #bringbackmonnett #firetacumah

The "Plan of Action"

"How am I supposed to perform my job well when I have so much opposition in the community?" Mrs. Tacumah lamented to her husband. "Being a teacher was so much easier than being a principal." She recalled that even her time as an AP was more rewarding than her time as the ASHS principal had been so far. Although the teachers and students have been very supportive of her, the whispers, pointing, and looks of disgust from unhappy community members at school games and elsewhere have been disconcerting and discouraging.

After reading the latest blog comments about herself and the petition against her, Mrs. Tacumah made an appointment with Dr. Gregory to discuss a plan of action for addressing the ongoing attacks. Despite her critics, Mrs. Tacumah has generally been happy at ASHS because, overall, people have been welcoming, friendly, and eager to have a collaborative leader. Even though the negative blog comments have had only a minimal effect on the school environment, she still wants to do something about them.

When the two administrators met, Dr. Gregory was surprised to hear that some individuals in the community were attacking Mrs. T through the *School Talk* blog, even though they did not really know her—and chose not to get to know her. The few community members who had complained to him at football games, Rotary Club meetings, church, and other places had no evidence to support their assertions. Furthermore, most of the complaints came from people who did not have any children attending ASHS. This phenomenon was a strange one, in his opinion, and he did not know exactly how to guide Mrs. T toward a positive resolution. The plan of action they decided on—to simply wait and ride out this insanity— was not much of a plan and did not involve much action. And if it were true that city council members were getting involved, their influence was likely to be felt at the school board meeting on December 11. The board president did ask Dr. Gregory to meet with him before then so that they could discuss Mrs. T's future at ASHS. Dr. Gregory was determined to fight to keep her as the ASHS principal and to demand that her sterling career not be blemished by unfounded accusations.

WHAT ELSE DO I NEED TO KNOW?

The following is a brief insight into the issues presented in the case study, with a brief literature review to help give context to those issues.

Slander, Libel, and Social Media

Curiosity from the school community (i.e., students, parents, other educators) about new persons on a campus is something to be expected.

Trying to find out what a new educator's interests are, for example, is usually done through questions from a school community who just want to get to know the "new guy." New educators on a campus may be asked whether they are married, whether they have children, whether they are religious, and whether they have a political preference. Although these questions can be seen as an invasion of privacy, typically, the point of the questions is to find out how the new educator will fit within the school family.

The high visibility of educators also brings this curiosity, because educators, in a sense, are public figures. As a public figure, one may think that it is your duty to answer questions from curious school community members, to be sure that you measure up to standards. Sadly, when school community members do not get answers, or at least the ones they expect to hear, they may begin to create answers, or "talk" about an educator.

Hence, the high visibility of educators is much like being a celebrity, and to some students and parents, educators' lives should be an open book; educators, after all, are working with others' children.

For those educators who experience talk that is slanderous or libelous, keep in mind the following. First, many courts have ruled that expressing negative opinions about persons in high-visibility positions, such as school administrators and other educators, is not illegal as long as the opinions are factual and do not interfere with those persons' job duties. Thus, school administrators and other educators whose jobs are inherently high profile must accept that teachers, students, and parents are free to criticize them. Not all high-profile educators accept this freedom of critics.

For instance, an influx of lawsuits has been levied by coaches against parents due to "...defamation, false light, invasion of privacy, intentional infliction of emotional distress, and malicious prosecution" (Green, 2014, p. 11). In 2009, one case in Connecticut involved a high school swim coach successfully winning an $88,000 judgment against a swimmer's mother who falsely alleged that the coach was a pedophile; whereas in 2005, a Chicago high school baseball coach won an $800,000 judgment after a parent fabricated and sent fake press releases to print and broadcast media outlets falsely claiming the coach was under investigation by the state's high school association for inappropriate coaching practices (Green, 2014). These examples show that some highly visible or high-profile educators are not accepting that nothing can be done about slander and libel.

If an educator wishes to sue someone for defamation, certain criteria must be met. Plaintiffs in a slander or libel suit must show that their reputation has been sullied, their ability to perform their job duties has been made more difficult, and their ability to gain another job has diminished. Consider that when a person makes the decision to sue another for defamation, McDaniel (2002) affirmed that

...that one individual may not harm another's reputation by false statements about his or her character....When words unjustly impute to another such qualities as immorality, vice, or dishonorable conduct, resulting in a loss of respect or esteem in the community, there may be grounds for a defamation suit. (pp. 34–35)

Examples of such cases where slander or libel lawsuits made it to the courts include *Blue Mountain School District v. Snyder* (2012); *Layshock ex rel. Layshock v. Hermitage School District* (2012); *Jerri Sharpton v. Blanca and Eddie Diaz* (2011); and *Draker v. Schreiber* (Texas Appeals—San Antonio, 2008).

Keep in mind that some parents and students may simply not like educators whose job includes disciplining students. Those disciplinarians may be called unflattering names, and rumors about them may start after a student is disciplined. Unless such criticism and rumors affect the learning environment and the administrator's ability to keep order on a campus, little can be done without possibly making the situation bigger and worse. And even if unfounded criticism from one parent is addressed, other parents may take his or her place. As high-profile persons, educators learn to have strong spines and thick skin.

When it comes to blogs, Twitter, Facebook, and other social media, it is best to follow state laws and school district policies if you are faced with online defamation. Some states address electronic communication through their educational or penal codes, which school districts uphold through their employee and student handbooks. Codes regarding electronic communications are not as stringent as they should be, however, because these media are relatively new and continually evolving.

What social media open up—specifically for slander and libel to occur—is that no longer is the school community confined to the school building; it now includes the peripheral outsiders in cyberworld. These peripheral outsiders are given chances to communicate their likes or distaste of a person purely based on a social media friend's insight. This expansion of the school community can cause defamation to have the potential of coming from persons who have and never will meet the person they are defaming.

"Cyberspace is not an area where laws do not apply...it is easy to say something in poor taste online, without seeing or appreciating the emotional consequences of an action" (Gillespie, 2012, p. 369). This is what occurs when a community of bloggers reacts to a principal without having all the facts; emotions compel poor taste.

Social media encourage slander and libel: slander, through videos and spoken dialogue, and libel, through anything in print. More social defamation lawsuits are on the horizon, which confirms two things: There are more opportunities for individuals to be victims of social defamation through the use of an online environment, and the laws have not caught up to the many violations of poor taste through the internet (i.e., victim, Internet service provider, and sender of information may be in different jurisdictions; Hiroko, 2013).

Outside Influences

Do outsiders, such as city council members, have an impact on a school district? Although outside parties may sometimes have an indirect impact on a district's policies and decisions, such outsiders do not have the legal authority to force their wishes on a school board.

In this case study, some community members view Mrs. Tacumah as an outsider, not only because she came from another city but because she replaced a local icon. They perceive her as a threat to the status quo, and they believe that her relative unfamiliarity with the community makes her incapable and undeserving of leading ASHS. For Mrs. T—and any educator who is new to a campus or district—the best antidote to such fears and criticism is visibility, through frequent and public interaction with community members. The following suggestions could be elements of an action plan to help an incoming educator gain the community's acceptance:

- Attend community events, participate in charitable fundraisers, patronize local shops and restaurants, and visit various churches.
- Join and be active in local organizations to show a desire to be a positive influence within the community. For example, volunteering at a local food bank will demonstrate an educator's caring and compassion, and joining the ethnic organizations represented within the community will demonstrate support of and commitment to cultural diversity.
- When participating in community activities, always be genuine and transparent. Educators who enjoy their role outside the school as much as their role within it will not feel forced or insincere as they go about making themselves more visible.

NCZ—NO CONSEQUENCE ZONE

Answer the questions below by applying what you know about this case and thinking about the steps you would take if you were faced with this situation or a similar one.

1 New superintendents routinely are tasked with making changes in their school district. Frequently they are given carte blanche to bring in their own people to lead schools or departments at the central office

level. This hiring freedom is usually a bargaining chip that an incoming superintendent negotiates before accepting the position.

    a. How did Dr. Gregory's change of principal at ASHS affect the school and the community?

    b. What were the social and political implications of that decision for Dr. Gregory?

2 New principals always have some obstacles to overcome, even if they have previously held a position in campus administration.

    a. What were the immediate obstacles that Mrs. Tacumah faced when she began her principalship?

    b. What are the obstacles for her after four months on the job?

    c. What might be obstacles for her as she nears the end of the school year and starts her second year at ASHS?

3 Persons who incite havoc on social media and make personal attacks online can be difficult to deal with, especially if they are anonymous.

    a. How should new principals handle lies or miscommunications about their experience or why they were hired?

    b. What should Mrs. Tacumah do about the false accusations made about her in comments on the *School Talk* blog?

    c. Should the teachers at ASHS try to do anything about the attacks being made on Mrs. Tacumah on the *School Talk* blog? If so, what might they do?

4 Being a new administrator on a campus and within a school district can be both exciting and intimidating. Introducing your own philosophy and ideas may be more easily accomplished if you encourage collaboration with and among the administrative staff and teachers.

    a. How can Mrs. Tacumah (or any new educator) acclimate successfully to the campus and the district?

    b. How could the assistant principals at ASHS go about informing Mrs. Tacumah of their duties and the campus procedures under the former principal? How can Mrs. Tacumah gain the trust of the APs, and what steps could she take to help them adjust to any new expectations she has of them?

    c. What can teachers do to help a new principal fit in with the established culture on a campus?

    d. What can a new principal do to be accepted as part of an existing campus family?

5 Now consider some big-picture questions about this case.

    a. What lasting effects might the ill will of the complaining community members have on Mrs. Tacumah and her career?

    b. Could the actions of the parents and other community members who are opposed to Mrs. Tacumah as principal have any negative consequences for them?

c. How would you expect a similar situation to play out in your own district and community?

REFERENCES

Gillespie, A. (2012). Twitter, jokes, and the law. *The Journal of Criminal Law*, 76(5), 364–372.

Green, L. (2014). Coaches suing parents of athletes. *School Administrator*, 71(10), 11.

Hiroko O. (2013). The online defamation maze: Are we finding a way out? *International Review of Law, Computers & Technology*, 27(1–2), 200–212.

McDaniel, T. R. (2002). Keeping defame from costing defortune. *The Education Digest*, 68(3), 34–37.

Chapter 4

The Cheerleaders and the Prank

Gender roles among students have changed a lot since most educators were themselves students at the primary level. There have been countless news stories that depict female students as less than the stereotype: sweet as spice and everything nice. Movies and TV shows have shown girls to be conniving, relentless, and calculating. Although these groups of girls are a minority, they have given schoolgirls a general, harsh reputation. Additionally, some girls today are no longer afraid of being labeled with unflattering names or having a reputation that gives them a fragile social status among their peers. Instead, recent news stories have featured girls who seek notoriety in whatever way is quickest. Additionally, some reported incidents have involved female students who appear to have no emotional affect or concern for others. Such attitudes in female students who are self-absorbed and eager to become infamous can create dangerous situations for students who share a campus with them. While boys can be described in the same way, the following case focuses on a group of girls who take a prank too far.

THE CASE

The Middle School and Its Reputation

Wayne Middle School (WMS), a campus of about a thousand students in grades six through eight, has long had the reputation of being the middle school with the problem parents and students. Specifically, WMS has been known for parents who bring lawyers to parent-teacher conferences, who regularly serve subpoenas to teachers when family custody battles emerge, and who file lawsuits against teachers and administrators when they feel wronged (for example, when they or their children do not get special treatment). Following their parents' examples, some students regularly threaten to sue teachers and administrators, refuse to follow the Student Code of Conduct, and feel entitled to have their own way. Although WMS is not an affluent school, its students and their parents behave as if money is no object.

Because of this challenging environment, WMS has a rapid and constant turnover of teachers and administrators. Each year, more than half of the staff requests a transfer. New teachers are regularly assigned to WMS because no one else wants to be in such an antagonistic and litigious environment. The administration sees changes annually, with at least one new administrator taking the place of an exiting one. Few principals stay longer than fifteen months and, in the last seven years, a succession of five principals have served WMS. The two assistant principal (AP) positions tend to keep persons a bit longer than the principals, but the school has a hard time keeping them, too. This school year has started with a new principal, Ms. Barnes; the two APs start their second year this school year.

The superintendent and the school board are not very supportive of the staff at WMS, at least that is the perception of those at WMS. They see WMS as an embarrassment, yet the leaders at the central office and on the school board seem unable to help the staff at WMS to improve the campus environment. Some WMS parents influence the central office administrators and the school board members by giving them special treatment and favors. For example, the deputy superintendent went car shopping at the local Mercedes dealership, which is owned by a WMS parent who is prominent in the community, and the administrator got such a discount on a new car that he felt indebted to the parent. Now whenever the parent has an issue regarding his son at WMS, he immediately calls the deputy superintendent, who then calls the administrators at WMS and demands that they resolve the issue in the way the parent wants.

So, this year appears to be like all the rest. The WMS staff is anxious with the new principal starting, but they are happy to see the two APs returning. They are also nervous about the students whom they will have this year, as parents have made it so difficult to enjoy their jobs. Too much litigation, and the threat thereof, have the staff second-guessing everything that they do.

The New Assistant Principal

This school year began as it usually does, with everyone eager to have a good year. As the year progressed, however, an angry parent filed a bogus lawsuit against an AP, claiming that the administrator had had sexual relations with his daughter. Although no concrete evidence pointed to a sexual affair and the daughter later confessed that she and her friends had made up the entire story, the AP was nevertheless encouraged to resign due to the optics. Even though he was found innocent of all charges, his name was tarnished in the education world, so he luckily found a corporate job. His resignation from WMS created a vacancy that needed to be filled immediately, and the principal hoped that the new AP could start before the Christmas break.

After a thorough but rushed search, the principal and her interviewing committee chose a new AP. Mr. Kibben had taught for fourteen years at the middle school level in a nearby school district, starting out as a speech and debate teacher and then teaching technology. With a goal of becoming an AP, he had just completed his master's degree in educational administration and received his state certification. He had hoped to serve as an AP within his former school district, but when the position opened at WMS, he felt it was kismet. This opportunity would provide him a chance to make more money and get closer to his goal of becoming a principal in a few years. It also meant that his wife could stay at home with their new twin babies. Regardless of the poor reputation of WMS, Mr. Kibben was determined to put in his time there and then move to a better school in a year or two.

The FEAR Cheer

The FEAR Cheer is a group of rebellious cheerleaders who dominate the school. They disregard the rules, bully other students, and even bully teachers whom they view as weak. The FEAR Cheer began about five and a half years ago when a group of the eighth-grade girls made the cheerleading squad. This clique vowed to create a school environment where girls ruled the campus and outshone the boys. The moniker "FEAR Cheer," or "FC" for short, came into being after these girls were involved in several incidents in which they mercilessly picked on other, more vulnerable students. They would regularly surround one student at a time in a hallway, bathroom, or classroom and yell at, hit, and spit on the cornered student until he or she cried and begged them to stop. The FC girls are proud to be a part of such an elite group, and they sport T-shirts, hats, jackets, purses, and jewelry emblazoned with the initials "FC."

The parents of the FC girls are proud of them, believing that their daughters are on their way to becoming strong feminists who will eventually attend an all-female college or university such as Smith or Wellesley. Like their daughters, the parents use bullying tactics when talking with teachers or administrators. They feel they can get their way because the superintendent's daughter was one of the founders of the original FC. Superintendent Lancit supported her daughter's strength in not allowing anyone to bully her or "put her in her place" while she was a WMS student three years ago, and Dr. Lancit still supports the FC today.

The coach of the current FC girls is Ms. Veale, a new teacher and coach in her first year of teaching at WMS. After Ms.Veale was hired, she was asked by the principal to coach the cheerleaders because no one else wanted to. Before she could answer, she was reminded that being a sponsor of a student group would help her earn a teaching contract for the following year. Ms./Coach Veale reluctantly accepted, especially after hearing that she would be the seventh cheer coach in five years.

Three weeks before Christmas break, basketball season was in full swing, and the FC was determined to do something that would make this year's squad legendary. As little to no discipline is imposed on the FC, each year the squad pledges to do one outrageous act to provoke the school administration to react and their parents to slap a lawsuit. Two years ago, the eighth-grade FC girls claimed to have stolen $1,500 worth of bras from a high-end department store by taking them off the rack, going to the dressing rooms to put them on under their clothes, and then walking out of the store. As they were clever enough to wear caps and undistinguishable clothing and avoid cameras and store clerks, no crime could be proved, and they escaped punishment.

Last year, the FC girls entered a sex shop while wearing their cheer outfits. They took items off the shelves, posed in questionable positions with them, and snapped photographs that they later posted on social media. When the shop owners asked them to leave, they ran, knocking over shelves on their way and damaging merchandise in the process. It was rumored that the girls' parents paid off the shop owners to keep them from filing any charges. The girls were not punished at school either, except for receiving demerits from the cheer coach. However, after the parents contacted the superintendent's office and succeeded in having the demerits removed and the cheer coach relieved of her duties, it was clear that the FC had gotten away with yet another prank.

This year, the FC girls had a plan that would top all past pranks and elevate them to eternal notoriety. Their prank was to take place before an eighth-grade boys' basketball game where they were to cheer. At one game, as the players were stretching and hanging out in the gym before the game, the FC took note that Marco, the team's manager and fellow classmate, was in the athletic cage, putting basketballs away. Marco was a bright student who was small for his age and mostly kept to himself, but he enjoyed helping the basketball team as their manager.

Nine girls approached Marco in the athletic cage, closed the cage door, and surrounded him. As the basketball players and coaches were preparing for the game in the gym, the FC girls began to tease Marco about his sexual desires and prowess, they made grand sexual overtures, and began to touch his buttocks, groin, and mouth. The girls took their turns at restraining and muffling him with deep kisses, while others removed his clothing and began to kiss him and make hickeys all over his body. Two girls stood and took pictures and video of the whole incident, in case they would need to prove what they did as the most unforgettable FC stunt ever. Their goal was to leave one hundred hickeys on Marco. After seven grueling minutes, the girls quickly and stealthily exited the athletic cage, unnoticed. Marco was left to recover from the attack and think about what his next step would be.

Marco was embarrassed and did not know how to handle reporting what had happened without being seen as a wimp or as not liking having so many girls' attention. The FC girls felt confident that their prank would go unreported and would definitely make WMS history. The basketball game began, but without Marco, who escaped the school grounds without being seen. He walked the two miles to his house, trying to take an inconspicuous route. Marco knew that his parents would not be home until after his bedtime, so he was able to shower and get to bed without their seeing all the bright red hickeys that covered his body from head to toe.

The Aftermath

The next day, the FC girls came to school bragging about what some "lucky guy" had received from them, even showing pictures of Marco's body on their phones. The girls thought they were smart, because they were not going to e-mail, text, or distribute the pictures or videos to anyone; they would just invite students to come look at their phones to view their awesome prank. In each picture and video, the cheerleaders had covered Marco's face, so his identity was not discovered. They never mentioned Marco's name, but they hinted that he was the boy with "love bites" all over his body. Coach Veale heard of the supposed FEAR Cheer prank and, when she asked the cheerleaders to see the pictures or videos, they told her, "Go eat a chainsaw!"

One of Marco's friends, Ted, who was on the basketball team, noticed that Marco had disappeared before the game started the previous night. The coaches asked Ted whether he knew where Marco had gone, but Ted did not know. The next morning, Ted stopped at Marco's house on his way to school. No one answered his knock on the door, so he tried calling both the house phone number and Marco's cell number, but he still did not get an answer. When Ted reached the school, he heard the rumor about what the FC girls had done to a "lucky guy." Ted looked for his friend, and after finding no sign of him, he decided to report Marco missing to his assigned AP, Mr. Kibben.

Mr. Kibben had heard about the FC long before coming to Wayne Middle School, but he did not think Marco could be in any danger. Nonetheless, after listening to Ted, he immediately called into Marco's scheduled class and was told by the teacher that Marco was not present. Like Ted, Mr. Kibben got no answer when he called Marco's home, but he was able to reach Marco's mother at her work number. She explained that she and her husband had gotten home late the night before and that when they checked on Marco, he was fast asleep in bed. They did not see Marco in the morning and thought that he had already left for school.

Mr. Kibben explained that Marco was not on campus and that his best friend, Ted, was worried because of the rumor that was being spread by the FC. The AP asked Marco's mother to meet him at her house, along with the school resource officer (SRO). Upon entering the home, they found Marco and were horrified at the sight of the bright red hickeys covering his body. When they asked him what had happened, Marco refused to answer. The boy's parents were very upset and demanded that charges be brought against the assailants. They also demanded that the SRO arrest the assailants, but the SRO needed a statement from Marco to pursue the case. Although Marco refused to name the FC girls as his assailants, Mr. Kibben had Ted's statement about Marco leaving the basketball game early, along with the now well-traveled rumor, as evidence that led to the FC. Mr. Kibben promised that something would be done from the school administration's side.

Heading back to campus, Mr. Kibben and the SRO discussed which sections of the Student Code of Conduct (SCOC) and the penal code had been violated, and they prepared to go to the principal with a plan of action to discipline and possibly arrest the FC squad. With the photographs and videos, they both felt that there would be enough evidence to move forward, but neither had seen this evidence and were not sure whether anyone would share them. They also needed to gather more statements from different students and call in the members of the FC to see whether any would break their silence. As the girls were openly bragging about the attack, Mr. Kibben and the SRO thought that someone would provide them with the pictures and videos that many students claimed to have seen. Mr. Kibben hoped that Marco would feel more comfortable providing a statement about who had assaulted him if there was concrete proof.

Mr. Kibben has much to think about. First, his principal, Ms. Barnes, is new and has already voiced concerns about coming back next year. She has had a couple of run-ins with some FC parents for supporting the coach who benched two cheerleaders who did not make the grade over the last six weeks. These parents complained to the superintendent and insisted that Ms. Barnes be fired. Second, the superintendent made it very clear in an e-mail at the beginning of the school year that all FC cheerleaders should be given special consideration before being disciplined for any reason. She also instructed that she be contacted before any discipline is administered. Yes, Mr. Kibben has a lot to think over before he takes action.

WHAT ELSE DO I NEED TO KNOW?

The following is a brief insight into the issues presented in the case study, with a brief literature review to help give context to those issues.

Assault and Sexual Assault

Many state penal codes address crimes involving assault and sexual assault. An assault is a threat or physical contact that is offensive or harmful. In the Texas Penal Code Chapter 22, assault is defined as the following:

a. a person commits an offense if the person:
   1. intentionally, knowingly, or recklessly causes bodily injury to another, including the person's spouse;
   2. intentionally or knowingly threatens another with imminent bodily injury, including the person's spouse;
   3. intentionally or knowingly causes physical contact with another when the person knows or should reasonably believe that the other will regard the contact as offensive or provocative.

For a verbal attack to be considered an assault, the victim must believe that a physical assault is imminent, and imminent is the key word. According to the Florida Statute, Chapter 784 on Assault, Battery, and Culpable Negligence, verbal assault is defined:

> An "assault" is an intentional, unlawful threat by word or act to do violence to the person of another, coupled with an apparent ability to do so, and doing some act which creates a well-founded fear in such other person that such violence is imminent.

Therefore, an assault occurs between at least two people and involves a threat or direct contact with the victim's body.

Sexual assault, then, is defined, in part, by the Michigan Penal Code 750.520b:

1. A person is guilty of criminal sexual conduct in the first degree if he or she engages in sexual penetration with another person and if any of the following circumstances exists:
   a. That other person is under 13 years of age.
   b. That other person is at least 13 but less than 16 years of age and any of the following:
      i. The actor is a member of the same household as the victim.
      ii. The actor is related to the victim by blood or affinity to the fourth degree.

iii. The actor is in a position of authority over the victim and used this authority to coerce the victim to submit.

In Arizona, the definition for "without consent", as outlined in Title 13 of the Sexual Offense Laws, includes:

a. The victim is coerced by the immediate use or threatened use of force against a person or property.
b. The victim is incapable of consent by reason of mental disorder, mental defect, drugs, alcohol, sleep or any other similar impairment of cognition and such condition is known or should have reasonably been known to the defendant. For purposes of this subdivision, "mental defect" means the victim is unable to comprehend the distinctively sexual nature of the conduct or is incapable of understanding or exercising the right to refuse to engage in the conduct with another.
c. The victim is intentionally deceived as to the nature of the act.
d. The victim is intentionally deceived to erroneously believe that the person is the victim's spouse.

Sexual assault in Arizona, therefore, occurs when a person intentionally or knowingly engages in sexual intercourse or oral sexual contact with any person without consent of such person. In some states, contact with the breasts does not constitute a sexual assault, but such contact would still be considered a regular physical assault.

When a minor has been assaulted, either the child or the parents must bring the charge to the police, who ultimately will seek a first-hand witness statement. When an assault occurs at home, parents may file on behalf of the minor child, but after a child has reached the age of seventeen or eighteen, the child's witness statement is essential. Even if the child and the parent refuse to report an assault or a sexual assault, the school may bring charges against the aggressor (for example, the cheerleaders in this case study) if the incident took place on campus or during a school-sponsored trip (such as a football game) based on violations of the Code of Conduct. For instance, if a student punches another student in the face, an administrator may file criminal charges against the aggressor for assaulting another person, with or without the cooperation of the victim. Conversely, for police to file assault charges against the same student, the student who was assaulted would have to cooperate (in most states, unless it was a family member by definition). Furthermore, when pictures or videos are posted in a public forum, such as a social media site, they become public information and, therefore, the school may pursue administrative charges.

When several assailants attack one victim, each assailant is considered separately as one person individually committing the assault on the victim. Many states do not recognize group crime, unless it falls under the organized-crime statute or the gang activity laws. Also, each state has its own codes relating to premeditation or malice aforethought: Did the accused commit a crime with malice? Did the accused have time to think about the consequences of the crime before committing it?

In sexual assault cases, the age of the victim is important, as different ages bring different statutes into play. If an eighth grader, such as Marco, has been sexually assaulted, a question that must be asked is, "Does the victim have the ability to give sexual consent?" The answer depends on the age of consent as outlined in your state's penal code. Some states have seventeen as the age of consent, whereas in other states, the age of consent may be much lower. Even if the assailant is the same age as the victim, the only age that matters is that of the victim. For all educators, it is prudent to know and understand what your state's criminal code specifies regarding assault and sexual assault and how the code aligns with your district's SCOC.

When it comes to sexual assault or sexual harassment in schools, research may help in understanding how to help both male and female students to cope. First, it has been found that females are primary victims, even though males have reported experiencing sexual assaults or harassment in schools (Henderson, 2008). Even when males are victims, according to Balogh, Kite, Picke, Canel, and Schroeder (2003), it was reported that males are less likely as compared to females to acknowledge that sexual harassment has occurred.

Second, Franiuk (2007) reported that sexual assault is underreported and that victims who choose not to report sexual harassment do so because they would like to "forget the experience, may not want to risk accusations of dishonesty, or may blame themselves for the incident" (p. 105). Many times, victims know their assailant, which also makes not reporting easier. Henderson (2008) found that those who experience sexual harassment, especially by the hand of someone whom they know at school, have reported feeling shame, fear, and embarrassment. This is reflected by talking less in class, staying at home, changing their regular routines, altering routes to and from school, and avoiding familiar places. Balogh et al. (2003) also found in their review of literature that those who encounter sexual harassment reacted through "somatic symptoms, decreased work performance, anxiety, depression, self-blame, anger, feelings of helplessness, fear of further or escalating harassment, and fear of retaliation for reporting the incident;" Male victims exhibited confrontational coping strategies when dealing with incidents of sexual harassment (p. 339)

Although sexual assaults and harassment can occur at any level in public schools, Young, Grey, and Boyd (2009) found that sexual assaults occurred more often in high schools, and the authors advocate for a relationship or dating violence prevention program, which may decrease or stop assaults altogether. These types of programs are most effective when they focus on non-dating acquaintance relationships (p. 1,082). Moreover, schools may inadvertently perpetuate the presence of sexual assault and harassment. In an article by Banyard, Moynihan, and Crossman, (2009), it was reported that schools create a risk environment due to the large population of students on one campus. With a sea of students constantly filling the halls, classrooms, bathrooms, and other covert places, it becomes easy for one student to be cornered by another and for an assault to occur.

Assaults can also be defined as a form of bullying, and this form of bullying can become accessible through the Internet. Shariff and Johnny (2007) define bullying as always being "unwanted, deliberate, persistent and relentless. Victim blame appears to justify social exclusion from the peer group"; therefore, cyberbullying is hidden or covert and it is "insidious and anonymous because perpetrators are shielded by screen names" (p. 311). Additionally, they found that the bully usually gains more support than the victim the longer that bullying persists. The reason, as the authors explain, is due to the bystanders: The longer the bullying occurs, the more bystanders will take notice. On the Internet, a covert bully can encourage other covert bullies to join in on the harassment of another, and those who may fear bullying at school, will see it easier to bully covertly and anonymously from their computer. This gives them power that they otherwise do not have. As the FC did not post pictures on the Internet, could they still be considered to be cyberbullying?

Further, although some schools do have character education and bullying policies implemented, rarely do these implements reach the complexities of cyberbullying (Shariff & Johnny, 2007). Usually, schools do a great job of defining, talking about, and identifying instances of bullying, but rarely do they dig deeper to what it really looks like when a bully bullies others and what the ramifications can be (i.e., libel, legal action). Barnes, Cross, Lester, Hearn, Epstein, and Cowan (2012) posited that covert bullying behaviors are invisible to educators, because overt bullying behaviors are easier to see and address. Additionally, schools rarely allow students to set the bullying prevention agenda, which may have educators missing the mark totally for their group of students. When it comes to online bullying, each state has its own set of laws, and each school district its own set of policies. When cyberbullying is suspected, Shear (2015) suggests that law enforcement should be involved due to the significant First Amendment issues that may be present. One other thing to note here is that often times persons using the Internet to bully will create online aliases, so as to give the appearance that other people support their position/bullying.

Outside Influences

State and federal codes mandate that parents must be a part of their children's education. Laws such as No Child Left Behind and the Individuals with Disabilities Education Act outline what parental involvement should look like on a campus and how educators should work with parents to help a child's academic achievement. At what point, however, do parents overstep their bounds and begin to harm their child's education? And at what point must administrators support the majority of the school rather than a small minority who consistently break the rules?

Many educators have seen how a school board member or even a superintendent is influenced by people in the community. In many states and cities, school board members are elected, and superintendents are appointed, so it is not surprising that those persons may want to appease the community members who have elected them or influenced their appointment. It is also natural that those who make the tough decisions for a school district want to be liked within their community. Superintendents would like to hold on to their position as long as possible, so being liked and being perceived as doing a good job are important to them. Unfortunately, making friends with and "getting on the good side" of those who can affect an election or an appointment may become the main goal of some educators and school board members.

How do other educators work with such persons? How does a principal, an AP, or a teacher encourage students to be successful and understand morals and ethics when other educators and some parents display the opposite of what students should learn? This is the fine line of politics in both administration and teaching: working toward keeping your job and earning a contract for the next year without upsetting anyone who could veto that contract, while simultaneously following the ethical and moral codes for educators as established by state and federal laws and doing what is best for *all* students and educators on a campus.

NCZ—NO CONSEQUENCE ZONE

Answer the questions below by applying what you know about this case and thinking about the steps you would take if you were faced with this situation or a similar one.

1 The SCOC should have a section that focuses on violations that are also penal code offenses, such as assault or sexual assault. These types of violations are arrestable offenses, and students who commit them are usually sent to an alternative education placement. Review your state's code and your school's SCOC, and then answer the following questions.
      a. What violations did the girls in the FC squad commit according to your state's and school's codes? What would be your plan of action for disciplining the girls?

  b. Would the girls be arrested, and if so, what must be done for their arrest to occur?

  c. What are the expellable offenses listed in your SCOC? Would the FC's actions lead to expulsions for the cheerleaders?

2 The SCOC and the state penal code usually define groups of students who are involved with criminal activity on a campus and in the community.

  a. What are your state's definitions of a gang, a sorority, a fraternity, and a secret society?

  b. Does the FC fall into this category of defined groups? Could the FC be subject to additional punishments beyond those specified by the SCOC?

3 The partnering of educators with parents is essential to student success in both academic and civic responsibility.

  a. How do the educators on a campus help to create a school environment wherein educators and parents are partners, not adversaries?

  b. Considering what happened to Marco in this case study, what steps need to be taken at the campus level to ensure that all students at the school are safe and that they receive the same, consistent, fair treatment when they violate the rules? Do any of these steps need to be implemented on your campus, too? What steps would parents be able to share in implementing?

4 Now let us look at the ripple effects of the incident described in this case study.

  a. How do you think Marco and his family will be affected emotionally and socially by the incident? What supports are available to help them recover?

  b. How will other students on the campus be affected?

  c. What are the social, emotional, and political implications for the coaches, the administrators, and the SRO?

  d. What consequences could the members of the FC who participated in the attack experience? How do you think this event will affect their future?

  e. How might a similar event play out differently in your school and your community?

REFERENCES

Arizona Revised Statute, Title 13, Chapter 14§13-1401 (2015)

Balogh, D. W., Kite, M., Picke, K., Canel, D., & Schroeder, J. (2003). The effects of delayed report and motive for reporting on perceptions of sexual harassment. *Sex Roles*, 48(7/8), 337–348.

Banyard, V., Moynihan, M., & Crossman, M. (2009). Reducing sexual violence on campus: The role of student leaders as empowered bystanders. *Journal of College Student Development*, 50(4), 446-457.

Barnes, A., Cross, D., Lester, L., Hearn, L., Epstein, M., & Cowan, E. (2012). The invisibility of covert bullying among students: Challenges for school intervention. *Australian Journal of Guidance and Counseling*, 22(2), 206–226.

Florida Statute, Chapter 784§.011 (2014).

Franiuk, R. (2007). Defining and discussion sexual assault: A classroom activity. *College Teaching*, (55)3, 104–107.

Henderson, J. E. (2008). *Examining educators' perceptions of student-on-student sexual harassment using appreciative inquiry in an elementary school setting* (Doctoral dissertation). University of Phoenix, ProQuest, UMI Dissertations Publishing.

Michigan Penal Code 750.520b (2014).

Shariff, S., & Johnny, L. (2007) Cyber-libel and cyber-bullying: Can schools protect student reputations and free-expression in virtual environments? *Education Law Journal*, 16(3), 307–342.

Shear, B. (2015). Five ways to keep social media from being a legal headache. *T H E Journal*, 44(8), 6–7.

Texas Penal Code, Title 5, Chapter 22§01 (2009).

Young, A., Grey, M., & Boyd, C. J. (2009). Adolescents' experiences of sexual assault by peers: Prevalence and nature of victimization occurring within and outside of school. *Youth Adolescence*, 38, 1072–1083.

Chapter 5

Beer, Bad Judgment, and Facebook

Employee privacy is something that campus and school district leaders should explain and describe to all employees at the start of each school year. It should be defined as to what it means and what actions would be considered violations. Specifically, clearly defined expectations for employees on how social media can be used should be outlined, including what is considered private information versus public information (i.e., some school districts do not allow for teachers to post where they work). In this case study, we meet a group of teachers who face big problems when their private actions are made public on Facebook—and an administrator who must respond. As a side topic, this case study also looks at how the death of a teacher affects an elementary campus.

THE CASE

The Principal and the Acclaimed Elementary School

Dr. Martin became the principal of North Briar Elementary (NBE) two years ago when he moved to the large suburban city of Briar Highlands. Because the student population at the school has increased each year, he has been given the okay to hire four additional teachers for his campus, including one to teach kindergarten. Dr. Martin called the new teachers into his office a week before school started to brief them on the district and campus policies and on his own expectations of teachers on his staff.

During the briefing, Dr. Martin emphasized that collaboration and teamwork are required of NBE teachers and that NBE's reputation for good teaching is extremely important, because it encourages the students to excel. Dr. Martin explained that the current teachers of NBE have implemented a team approach to everything they do. Working together as a team has brought the teachers closer to one another and fosters a familial atmosphere on campus. As a whole, the school family has become quite close and, in Dr. Martin's opinion, that closeness is a big reason why NBE has such a terrific reputation.

Word of mouth about NBE's dedicated staff has enticed many new families to move to Briar Highlands, raising student enrollment. NBE has also had many student transfer requests from across the district, and it is becoming quite large for an elementary school, with a current population of 932 students. Being a part of a growing school with new students each year is exciting for the staff. Despite NBE's stellar reputation, however, troubling rumors about some teachers' personal lives have recently been circulating. However, as the rumors have not directly affected the learning environment, Dr. Martin has chosen not to address them.

The Fifth-Grade Teaching Team

For about three years, the team of fifth-grade teachers at NBE have had a questionable reputation. They are all women in their twenties who are either married or in a relationship, but their relationship status does not prevent them from partying together controversially, according to the rumor mill. The teachers and their husbands and boyfriends allegedly meet at one of the teacher's homes routinely every Saturday to play a series of drinking games that result in everyone getting drunk. At midnight, the partner swapping supposedly begins, with either the men or the women drawing names from a bowl to determine with whom they will spend the rest of the night having sex, just as long as it is not their significant other. The next morning, each reunited couple goes home to sleep off their hangover.

At school on Mondays, the fifth-grade teachers are always upbeat and motivated to teach, and their enthusiasm lasts through the entire week. Even though many people have gossiped about the infamous Saturday nights, the teachers have never given anyone a spark of evidence to confirm the gossip. One of the main reasons why Dr. Martin and other administrators have not addressed the rumors is that even if the teachers have been partying on the weekends in private homes, at school they always behave as top-notch teachers. Additionally, the teachers have never spoken about these Saturday-night trysts, even when asked directly about them.

Recently, the rumormongers have expanded their stories to include parents who are allegedly being invited to the teachers' Saturday soirees. Supposedly, only a few select parent couples who have been vetted as interested, good-looking, and able to be discreet have been invited to join this secret society. Still, no actual evidence confirming the rumors has ever been linked to the teachers, and no one has lodged a complaint with Dr. Martin, the superintendent, or the school board.

When Dr. Martin first started at NBE, he was told about this rumor, but he quickly perceived that the fifth-grade teachers are exceptional educators whose students succeed in their coursework and consistently score in the upper ninetieth percentile on state assessments. Two of the teachers have won the school district's Teacher of the Year award, and one of them has been named Teacher of the Year by her teachers' association. Furthermore, this team of teachers is well respected by the school staff, the students, and the parents. Each year, the fifth-grade teachers are honored by their peers on campus as having the best-behaved students and the best-designed lesson plans for producing outstanding student achievement. Dr. Martin has assumed that surely teachers who merit such accolades could not be behaving unbecomingly during their personal time. Or could they?

A Campus Tragedy and a Vulnerable New Teacher

Dr. Martin had every reason to expect that his third year at NBE would be another impressive one that would further enhance the school's reputation. In January, however, things began to unravel at NBE. For instance, a pregnant kindergarten teacher, Mrs. Cantrell, was killed in a car accident on her way to school one morning. News of her death devastated the campus. Mrs. Cantrell had been an especially lively and supportive teacher and was missed very much.

Because of her natural teaching ability and her successes with students, Mrs. Cantrell had been appointed to mentor the new kindergarten teacher, Ms. Price. The relationship was a fruitful one, and Ms. Price felt lucky that she was being guided by such a loved and masterful teacher. After her mentor died, Ms. Price was finding it difficult to get back into teaching.

On a Friday, five weeks after Mrs. Cantrell's death, two of the fifth-grade teachers found Ms. Price crying in the teachers' workroom and tried to comfort her. They listened to her lamenting the loss of the mentor she had learned so much from, and they tried to help her feel better about moving on and perfecting her craft as a teacher. Eventually, the two fifth-grade teachers invited Ms. Price to their Saturday gathering, and she accepted. Following her mentor's advice, Ms. Price had not paid much attention to rumors, so when she decided to attend the get-together, she thought it would be an innocent dinner with good conversation. She was happy about the prospect of getting to know new teachers to pal around with, and she looked forward to relaxing with colleagues who were so revered.

Arriving alone at the gathering, Ms. Price immediately recognized all the fifth-grade teachers and also identified three sets of parents she had seen on the campus. She had not been told that parents would be at the party too, so she was not sure whether she should stay. After the teachers welcomed her and said that the parents were "cool," she felt a little more at ease. Later, one of the teachers told her in private that the parents were a new addition to their Saturday-night parties, because the teachers' spouses and boyfriends wanted "fresh meat." Ms. Price did not understand this odd comment, but she thought it was probably an inside joke and did not question it.

During dinner, Ms. Price began to feel uncomfortable again, not only because she was the lone person there who was not in a couple but because the men began to flirt with her. She did not want to seem rude or ungrateful for her colleagues' hospitality, so she reluctantly stayed. After dinner, Ms. Price noticed that everyone was becoming inebriated and wanted to play games that involved even more drinking. These pursuits did not interest her, so she decided to leave, despite the many protests she received. On her drive home, Ms. Price concluded that although she would be friendly to the fifth-grade teachers at school, she would no longer meet with them socially.

A Fateful Evening

The rest of the night for the remaining partygoers was more rambunctious than ever, and the teachers did something they had never done before: They allowed photographs to be taken. One of the male parents wanted to take pictures of all the fun and of each of the twosomes as they went to separate rooms. He promised to keep the pictures private and to send them only to the participants but, in a stupor, he uploaded some of the risqué photos to Facebook early Sunday morning.

By Monday morning, the new rumor making the rounds led many teachers to check out the parent's Facebook page, where they saw unseemly photographs of the teachers, their husbands and boyfriends, and the parents drinking and in suggestive poses. Thankfully for Ms. Price, she was not in any of the photos. For many at NBE, this was disappointing and disheartening proof that the rumors floating around for the past three years were true. That a parent had been the one to post the pictures somehow made the confirmation even more distressing. The parent's ultimate goal seemed to be that he wanted to share the experience with other couples he knew, to entice them to start a swingers' club with him and his wife.

When the news hit the campus, Dr. Martin was at a meeting at the central office. As he was heading back to his car, he received a call from his secretary, advising him to take a look at the parent's Facebook page. Using his phone to find the webpage, Dr. Martin was stunned and sickened to discover that the rumors about the fifth-grade teachers were true after all. Sitting in his car in the central office parking lot, he pondered the situation and thought about what he would have to do next.

WHAT ELSE DO I NEED TO KNOW?

The following is a brief insight into the issues presented in the case study, with a brief literature review to help give context to those issues.

Teachers' Private Lives, Freedom of Speech, and Ethics

Can teachers be reprimanded by their administrators for things they have done in their private lives and in their private homes? Can a teacher be fired for something that happened in the past? Should a teacher be fired for violating school board policy regarding moral turpitude? Can teachers be fired for a pictures posted by another person on a popular social media website? And, do young teachers have an unfair bull's-eye on them? The answers to these questions are all related to the relationship between school districts and teachers. It must be remembered that educators are employees of a school district and that school districts may legally make policies that allow a contract to be terminated because of an employee's private activities once they become public. For young teachers,

> ...[they] have grown up in the cyber age and often do not recognize the boundaries between work and play that their more mature peers observed. Boundaries are more easily violated with social networking technology. What was once private is now very public. (O'Donovan, 2012, p. 34)

Regardless of age, all employees should distinguish between what is professional and what is not; this will help in recognizing the boundaries between work and play.

In cases that involve non-educators, the answers to the questions may seem clearer. In *San Diego v. Roe* (543 US 77 [2004]), for example, John Roe was a San Diego police officer who was fired for selling a sexually graphic video of himself on eBay. The video was sold through eBay's adults-only section and revealed Roe stripping off a police uniform and masturbating. Although he did not disclose his actual name, Roe identified himself as a police officer in his eBay profile, and his user name (code3stud@aol. com) was a play on words, since Code 3 was a high-priority police code in San Diego. After his superiors found out about this enterprise, Roe was fired from the police force for making and selling a video that showed him "engaging in sexually explicit acts." Given that the video was made in private and was sold privately, was Roe's termination a violation of his First Amendment right to free speech? Ultimately, the U.S. Supreme Court unanimously said no. As was partly established in *Connick v. Myers* (461 US. 138 [1983]), government employers may restrict employees' speech that is not of public concern without violating their First Amendment rights. Thus, the Supreme Court found that Roe's termination did not violate his rights, because his video was not a matter of public concern: that is, it did not help to inform the public about the police department, and it was also detrimental to the police force.

Our case study shares some similarities with the *San Diego v. Roe* case, as the teachers of NBE were photographed performing sexual acts in private. When the photographs were posted online, however, their private actions thereby became detrimental to the school and the district, and their ability to teach effectively became questionable. As in the *San Diego v. Roe* case, the teachers' actions did not involve a matter of public concern, so firing the teachers would not violate their right to free speech, right? Unfortunately for these teachers, social networking has opened "...a number of ethical vulnerabilities that may be unlike those encountered in other areas of the teaching profession." (Foulger, Ewbank, Adam, Popp, & Carter, 2009, p. 18)

Educators are held to a higher standard than most professionals because they are in constant contact with children. "The public often holds teachers to a higher moral and ethical standard than the general populace because they are mentors, coaches, and examples for the nation's youth" (Miller, 2011, p. 637). However, it is understood that educators are people who do have personal lives that are in parallel to their professional lives. Although parents do expect a much more stringent, higher standard from teachers, teachers will make mistakes. When it comes to any social media sites, mistakes can be made: "Facebook can make private conversations or social gatherings public—sometimes because of lapse of judgment on the teacher's part, and sometimes involuntarily or unwittingly" (Miller, 2011, p.639). Although teachers (and other school employees) will make mistakes, remaining diligent in holding that moral and ethical standard at all times will help lapses of judgment be few.

So, what is to be done about the use of social media by educators? Are there guidelines or procedures that can be emulated? In an article about health care education, a discussion on e-professionalism was a focus. As defined by Cain and Romanelli, e-professionalism is the "attitudes and behaviors ... reflecting traditional professionalism paradigms that are manifested through digital media"; this definition clearly describes a younger generation whose online identity plays a significant role in their professional lives (as cited in Yap & Tiang, 2014, pp. 26–27). Encouraging young educators to use social media responsibly by implementing policy that defines what responsibly means will help schools to have a decrease of problems concerning inappropriate information being posted on social media.

Additionally, Yap and Tiang (2014) suggested that those who do have online profiles and information posted on social websites should be careful as to what is displayed for all to see. Information about a person can be used to form opinions about that person, which may not be flattering and could be detrimental when seeking to keep a job. Furthermore, understanding that a post may have been meant to convey one message may not be the intended outcome. For example, sarcasm and teasing may not be evident from a post, and one may unintentionally perceive sarcasm and teasing as offensive, mean, and derogatory. Social media, then, is not always the best way to show the best qualities of oneself.

When educators' private lives interfere with the school environment, their actions may become an ethical issue. The school board and the school district have the right to establish policies regarding ethics and morals and consequences for violating those policies. The Educator Code of Ethics is usually defined at the state level, and school districts enforce it at the local level. Furthermore, many educator contracts state clearly that moral turpitude is grounds for dismissal. The contract may also specify actions that are considered unbecoming of an educator, as set forth by the school board. Many school districts have addressed educators' use of social media in particular, by placing guidelines about it in their employee handbooks and/or in educator contracts. Such guidelines usually list which actions could cause a contract termination. Note that a violation of ethics is not usually a criminal offense, unless the state has included criminal provisions within its Educator Code of Ethics.

Before an educator accepts a position within a school district, it is up to the educator to research and understand the expectations of the school board and what actions could lead to contract termination. Thus, actions that educators do at home in private and that do not affect their school or district in any way are constitutionally protected. Educators must remember, however, that private actions that become public and then hinder the educators' ability to perform their assigned job duties—or are detrimental to their employer—are not constitutionally protected.

Educators do have protection of their speech, but that protection is for speech that concerns matters of public interest; there is a connection between teachers' private speech, specifically on social media, and their employment at school (O'Donovan, 2012). Therefore, private speech should not unduly disrupt school activities.

Death in the Campus Family

The death of a teacher is one of the most difficult events that any campus will go through. For an administrator, personal grief is coupled with the need to carry out a special role, because everyone on the campus will look to the administrator for guidance, support, and acknowledgment of the death. There is no one right way to handle the death of any campus member, but when the member is a teacher, administrators may find the following suggestions useful for helping the campus grieve and move forward:

- Be transparent. Once you are informed of a teacher's death, immediately let the teaching staff know, in person. If possible, call a quick faculty meeting, so that they all hear the news at the same time and can console one another. In some cases, using a phone tree to disseminate information about a death may be the only avenue at the time.
- Tell the students. The administrators and staff should discuss the best way to tell the students about the death, especially those students who are currently in a course or class with the teacher. Being transparent and matter-of-fact with the students is a must so that they do not make wild guesses about what has occurred. Then, draft a letter that encapsulates what you told the students about the teacher's death and send it home to parents. Include the funeral details, if available, or a statement of where those details will be posted when known.
- Allow time to grieve. Once the staff and students know about the death, give them counseling opportunities and time to grieve. This time will vary among the campus family, but do not be surprised if the grieving lasts for weeks and months. Be patient and helpful in working with those who may need more intense counseling or interventions to cope with the death.
- Watch for signs of depression. Sometimes individual staff members or students may blame themselves or others for a teacher's death, and they may become depressed or even suicidal. Be on the lookout for students or educators who are behaving differently from their normal demeanor. It is paramount that you constantly observe those who are taking a longer time to grieve and that you talk with them and, as appropriate, their family members about your concerns.

The death of a teacher may affect school operations for some time, especially if the teacher was a part of a popular student activity. Ask for volunteers to take up the teacher's duties, and try to get activities back to normal as soon as possible. Additionally, many people will look to the administrator for the strength and guidance about how to proceed, so be diligent in your actions, words, and assistance. However, do give yourself time to grieve and accept the teacher's death.

More information on how to work through a death on a campus can be found in Chapter 11, The Jealous Shooter.

NCZ—NO CONSEQUENCE ZONE

Answer the questions below by applying what you know about this case and thinking about the steps you would take if you were faced with this situation or a similar one.

1 Most school districts have policies that address privacy issues and social media that are aligned to federal, state, and local laws and codes.
   a. Find out what your school district and campus policies are regarding social media and personal websites.
   b. Based on what you found, what kind of reprimand could be given to the teachers in this case study? What would be the school's approach toward the parent who posted the photos on Facebook?
   c. Does a principal have any jurisdiction over teachers or parents when an activity or action has taken place at a private home? Why or why not?
   d. When does an administrator have the right to recommend that a teacher's contract be terminated for actions done in private?
2 Many schools have been through the death of a teacher, a student, or another campus staff member.
   a. What action plan should be in place to help your campus family get through a teacher's death?
   b. Will the steps be different for the adults than for the students on the campus?
3 Now let us look at the bigger picture surrounding this case study.
   a. What are the social and political repercussions for the administrators and staff at North Briar Elementary? For the parents?
   b. How might a similar situation unfold in your own community?

REFERENCES

Foulger, T., Ewbank, A., Adam, K., Popp, S., & Carter, H. (2009). Moral spaces in myspace: Preservice teachers' perspectives about ethical issues in social networking. *Journal of Research on Technology in Education*, 42(1), 1–28.

Miller, R. (2011). Teacher facebook speech: Protected or not? *Brigham Young University Education and Law Journal*, 2011(2), 637–665.

O'Donovan, E. (2012). Social media: Guidelines for school administrators. *District Administration*, 2012(48), 34–36.

Yap, K. Y. & Tiang, Y.L. (2014). Recommendations for health care educators on e-professionalism and student behavior on social networking sites. *Medicolegal and Bioethics*, 2014(4), 25–36.

Chapter 6

The Online Fine Arts Academy

Online schools have become more prolific in the past few years, specifically, in public education. Online schools provide a different instructional delivery for non-traditional students, which make them so appealing to students and parents. Students who enjoy using technology and like the flexibility of what an online school can provide also seem to enjoy the freedom and responsibility of owning their learning. The following case highlights an online school but also shows how some students manipulate the online environment to test the waters of being daring using school e-mail accounts.

THE CASE

School within a School

The community of Bortzview lies within an urban school district whose educators and students come from a variety of cultural, religious, and ethnic backgrounds. Amid this diversity, the dominant cultural belief within the district is that technology can help everyone become successful. All schools are equipped with technology labs, and some schools have bought their students iPads or laptops, depending on the grants they have received. The district also is very interested in making online schools available for different types of students (i.e., an online school for the gifted and an online science, technology, engineering, and mathematics [STEM] school). This high level of interest in technology is due to the fact that Bortzview established itself several years ago as a technology center, and high-tech and other businesses have helped make it an affluent city that attracts families from around the nation. The number of building permits issued for new homes has tripled during the last four years, with a related increase in the student population at each campus in the district.

With 3,200 students, Winter Knoll High School (WKHS) is the largest of Bortzview's five high schools. It is a magnet school, housing the Online Estes Academy of Fine Arts (OEAFA) in one of its smaller wings; hence, OEAFA functions as a school-within-a-school. OEAFA is a fully online school, and the administrators and teachers of the school are housed at WKHS. Additionally, even though it is an online school, students must come to campus for performances and shows. The principal, the assistant principal, advisors/counselors, and the twenty-five teachers all have offices that they work from, and two classrooms are available for the occasional F2F meetings that some teachers enjoy having. The school has a band hall, a choir room, a dance studio, an art room, an auditorium with a pit and stage, and two computer labs. Although large groups of OEAFA students are seen only occasionally, the school-within-a-school is working for both WKHS and OEAFA staff and students.

Dr. Isabelle Laurent has been the principal of OEAFA since it has been open for business. Two and half years ago, she accepted the principalship of this online school because she believed that technology is the future. In her third year, she is so pleased with the success her students and staff have shown and she is proud of the fine arts students who have graduated and have been admitted in top universities. When the school district decided to create an online fine arts academy, many people voiced that it would be impossible for students to learn the art of performance online. Further, it was emphasized that performers needed the social interaction and without that interaction, how could a choir ensemble sing on key, the dance team work on an ensemble piece, or the symphony appreciate staying in tempo? Thankfully, the recent graduates have proved that obtaining fine arts scholarships to renowned fine arts schools is possible for an online student.

The other staff members who helped put OEFSA on the map are Mr. Richard Scheurich, assistant principal, five advisors/counselors, and fourteen curriculum and elective teachers, eleven fine arts teachers (i.e., dance, choir and voice, orchestra and jazz, theatre, and art), and three computer technicians. The state curriculum is followed but has been adapted for online learning. Those students who are in advanced courses or who wish to take college-level courses are encouraged to take fully online courses given through the local community college.

The Online Estes Academy of Fine Arts

The Estes Academy of Fine Arts has always been a dynamic school, where the staff helps to prepare students for graduation and a life of artistic pursuits. Generally speaking, its teachers tend to be territorial, flamboyant, and opinionated, and they expect superior performance from their students. Before students are accepted to study at OEAFA, they must go through a tough application process that includes a lengthy application, three separate interviews (with a teacher committee, a student committee, and an administrative committee), a two-page essay, a two- to five-minute solo presentation or performance in front of a select committee, and the submission of five recommendation letters, with a grade point average (GPA) of 3.5.

Once students have been admitted, they are expected to maintain a 3.5 GPA, to participate in all assigned performances and shows and to have satisfactory attendance and behavior records. If any of these expectations are not met, the student is put on probation for six weeks. If after this time the student is still not meeting expectations, he or she is dismissed from OEAFA. At the end of each year, the students must prove that they deserve to stay another year by having a one-to-one conference with their advisor/counselor and their advising teacher, in which they present a portfolio, a video, a live performance, or any other information that shows their growth. The advising teachers use a uniform rubric to evaluate each student. The academy's expectations of students are outlined in a contract that both the students and their parents must sign. The contract stresses that attending the academy is not a right but a privilege.

ONLINE ESTES ACADEMY OF FINE ARTS AT WINTER KNOLL HIGH SCHOOL

Student-Parent-Educator Contract

All who come through the doors of the Estes Academy of Fine Arts must heed the Estes motto:

Honor, respect, perform!

The OEAFA mission statement expands on this motto:

All who learn at the Online Estes Academy of Fine Arts are responsible for honoring all obligations and expectations, for respecting others by acknowledging diversity, and for performing to the best of their abilities.

The Honor Code helps all to adhere to a successful online learning environment and helps to promote a moral code that supports the mission.

The Honor Code

I will not lie, cheat, or steal, or tolerate anyone who does, and I will behave ethically and morally at all times.

Any violations of the mission or the Honor Code will result in dismissal from OEAFA, and other possible consequences that align with the Student Code of Conduct (SCOC) may be applied.

To be a part of the OEAFA family is a privilege. Accordingly, students and their parents must obey all rules, regulations, policies, and procedures enforced at the OEAFA for students to be allowed to attend the OEAFA. This contract complies with the policies of the Bortzview School Board.

To foster a rewarding educational experience for each OEAFA student, the persons signing this contract agree to adhere to the following OEAFA guidelines for students, parents, and teachers.

Students

1 I will not lie, cheat, or steal anything that pertains to my being unsuccessful online. I will submit only work that I have completed and that is of high quality. Each time I submit work online, I have electronically confirmed that I alone am the sole author of said work.
2 I will uphold the mission and the Honor Code or face the consequences of not doing so.
3 To be a member of the OEAFA family, I will make every effort to learn what is required of me and to apply my learning to my craft.
4 I will follow all rules and do what is expected of me at all times. I will not make excuses or expect special privileges.
5 If I have questions, I will promptly ask for assistance from my teachers and the technical staff. I will not wait until it is too late to ensure that I am excelling.
6 I will maintain a GPA of 3.5 or higher.
7 I will attend all assigned performances.
8 I will complete all daily online expectations and post them before the due dates given. NO excuses, such as technical or computer difficulties, will be honored. All difficulties must be taken care of before due dates. (Remember that OEAFA at Winter Knoll High School has two computer labs for all students to use at anytime.)
9 I will follow the Student Code of Conduct (SCOC) that has been approved by the Bortzview School Board and any other rules that are imposed by Winter Knoll High School and OEAFA.

continued ...

10 I understand that if I fail to meet any of the above expectations, I will be placed on probation for a minimum of six weeks. If after this time I am still not meeting the OEAFA's expectations, I will be dismissed from the OEAFA.

Parents

1 I will support my student at the OEAFA by becoming a positive partner with the academy's staff. I will make certain my current contact information is correct throughout the year, and I will be readily available for parent-teacher-student conferences that are held to help my student succeed.

2 I will ensure that my student follows and demonstrates the tenets of the mission and the Honor Code, and if he/she fails to do so, I will fully support OEAFA's consequences.

3 I will provide my student with a computer with the specifications outlined in the parent handbook. This computer will be for my student to use solely for work to be done for OEAFA. If I am unable to provide my child with a computer, I understand that my student may attend OEAFA at Winter Knoll High School and use a computer in one of their two computer labs.

4 I will ensure that my student has a quiet room in our home for preparing, practicing, and studying for each course and obtaining a GPA of at least a 3.5.

5 I will encourage my student to be his/her best and to strive to learn all that he/she can at OEAFA.

6 I will ensure that my student goes to school prepared and ready to learn.

7 I will help ensure that my student fulfills all OEAFA expectations and abides by the rules and the SCOC, and I will support the OEAFA educators and their decisions if my student chooses not to do so.

Teachers

1 I will contribute to an online school environment that is welcoming, safe, civil, and encouraging for each person who enters the OEAFA campus.

2 I will uphold the mission and the Honor Code and will not tolerate any defiance toward them.

3 I will be "visible" in the online course room each day from Monday through Friday from 9 to 3 p.m. daily, and I will be available for F2F (face-to-face) communications during this time.

4 I will respect all students and their aspirations, and I will support and assist students to develop their fine arts talent.

5 I will encourage students to strive to do their best and to maintain a GPA of 3.5 or higher.

6 Throughout the year, I will assign students to at least five performances and/or shows that they must attend. These performances may be at any high school within Bortzview. I will also ensure that transportation is available to and from each performance.

7 I will enforce the attendance expectations and the SCOC for all students. I will not give special treatment to any student, and I will expect the very best from each.

Student Signature	Printed Name	Date
Parent Signature	Printed Name	Date
Advising Teacher Signature	Printed Name	Date

THE ONLINE LEARNING PLATFORM

Due to the high expectations of the school and due to the culture of Bortview, the 1,500 online students have done very well. Most of the students of Bortzview have grown up in a family and world that included high levels of technology and, at times, the students have been able to teach the teachers—and even the techs—some tricks of the trade. For these students, online learning has been fabulous, because some have been able to establish private lessons with established fine artists around the world. One student was able to learn to play the bassoon in three months, due to the one-to-one private lessons she was able to secure with a German bassoonist in Nuremberg. Another student learned the art of a Japanese dance called Butoh by working with a student in Japan through Facetime. They were able to create a duet that they performed for their respective teachers by showing one dancer on a large screen by the way of Facetime as the other dancer danced the same dance in person.

The online school concept has been a success, even more so now, in its third year. The online learning platform used for the delivery of instruction is similar to all others, such as BlackBoard, except for one feature: the Student Café. This feature that can be used and seen only by students allows for students to have private conversations concerning the course work, but the teacher can be brought into a conversation when invited by a student. When the educators at OEAFA sought the best platform for online learning, the Student Café feature seemed a perfect way for the students to collaborate and work together without the interference of teachers, who may diminish creativity. Just as in an F2F environment, students need a quite place, without any intrusion from teachers, to collaborate and learn to work with others.

What makes this online academy successful is the dedication that the students, parents, and educators have in making the learning meaningful and well rounded. The students may work solely from home, but they have the opportunity to come to the campus each day of the week to work in one of the two computer labs set up purposefully for the students. Some have argued that having these labs defeats the purpose of online, because a truly online school is completed exclusively at home. The educators of OEAFA, however, have proven that even though the academy is fully online, having the option for students to come in for an occasional F2F class or to use a computer only helps the students. Additionally, for students and families who cannot afford the technology needed to be successful at OEAFA, the school's decision to provide computer labs instead of personal computers was twofold: It was easier to maintain and more cost effective to have the computers on campus, and it forced the students to come to campus.

When WKHS was built four years ago, the school district knew that they would offer a fully online school in the near future. Therefore, WKHS was built with a secondary area or campus that would house the online faculty. When the school district finally decided that a Fine Arts Academy would be the choice for the online academy, the school-within-a-school was built with fine arts halls, rooms, and studios needed to help the talented students improve on their gifts. So, when any teacher wanted the students to come to campus to practice or work toward a performance or show, they could come to a campus that was well equipped to meet their needs.

For example, even though the majority of the work is done online, students must come to campus to prepare for fall and spring performances or shows. The choir and orchestra students will practice their musical parts for a performance on their own, and even will Facetime or Skype with one another to practice certain parts. Dance is similar, in that the students are sent a video of a dance from their dance teacher that they will be responsible for learning at home, and then they will come to campus to work with partners or groups to perfect the dance. The theatre students are given a script and practice their lines at home but must come to campus to put a play together. For the art students, as some of them must use certain tools, such as a kiln, they usually come to campus and work on their artwork during the year. Hence, the students learn online but do have many opportunities to meet F2F throughout the year. In fact, any student who wishes to come to campus daily to work on a performance or show and use the computer labs to work on academic assignments is welcome. The students would check in with their advisor before going to a computer lab, where they would find teachers ready to help tutor or facilitate learning in the core subjects. The fine arts teachers would be in their respective areas, ready for any student who would come in for practices. Thus, the online learning environment coupled with the many opportunities for F2F with the staff of OEAFA gives more responsibility of learning to the students, more so than a "regular" campus would.

The Student Café

The students were doing so well at OEAFA that schools from all over the state were coming to observe how the first online fine arts academy was able to be so successful. The talent of each student was not in question, because each student had to perform or show their skills in person or in a video periodically, and there was not a way in which a student could deceive the teachers. The questions that came from visitors around the state, however, focused on how the core teachers could be certain that their students were the ones who submitted original work that was indeed theirs. The only answer that the faculty at OEAFA could give concerned the Honor Code, which is the first thing that everyone who entered the OEAFA campus saw on a banner strung across the foyer. Online, the code was visible on a banner that popped up on the homepage.

The Honor Code—*I will not lie, cheat, or steal, or tolerate anyone who does, and I will behave ethically and morally at all times*—was voted as a necessary tool by the staff and is literally taught through a course online. This course is the first one each student must take, and it focuses on the ethical and moral aspects of what it means to practice and adhere to the Honor Code and to working in an online environment. Activities such as solving ethical case studies and participating in discussions on current news stories that focus on lying, cheating, and stealing of intellectual and artistic property were created to help the students to practice understanding what it means to abide by the Honor Code at OEAFA. The educators trust that each student will rise to the high expectations of OEAFA because he or she believes in and practices the Honor Code.

This was a big reason for buying the educational platform with the Student Café feature. Students really seemed to like being able to work in peer groups both online and on campus. And, as the students needed or wanted, they could invite a teacher to their Student Café discussion by simply clicking a button. In fact, groups of students have invited the entire OEAFA campus to discuss certain topics; then the students wanted everyone to have a chance to voice their opinions. For example, when some students in psychology needed to complete an assignment that had them survey several people about their grooming habits, they decided to create a survey using the Student Café tools, and then they invited the entire campus to take the survey. This meant that everyone who was invited was able to see that groups' café area, specifically the survey. Because it was so easy to invite anyone who has an OEAFA e-mail address, the Student Café was the perfect feature for an online academy.

Some students agreed that the Student Café was an ideal tool to have online because it gave some of them an opportunity to try some things out, such as selling and buying things. Somewhat like an eBay or Amazon site, these students turned their Student Café into a purchasing site named COOL-Bay, ostensibly to earn some cash instead of getting a job. The "Original Five" students created a café area for themselves for the sole purpose to sell and buy items to and from other OEAFA students. They started off with seemingly harmless things like the following:

Student Café
COOL-Bay

Selling and Buying	*Contact*
Have an old trumpet I need to sell if anyone is interested.	Michael at 698-4781—call after 4PM
Need prom dresses from the 80's for a monologue I'm working on. Anyone have one?	Sue at 548-4759 I'M DESPERATE
Selling my tap and ballet shoes. They have only been worn twice. In great shape.	Tallia at 789-846
NEED to sell my freshman books for some extra cash.	If you are interested, call. Sam—I'm on campus every Tuesday and Thursday. Come find me. Vanessa—I have books to sell too—call me at 478-7894
Gotta get rid of my old jeans that don't fit anymore. If you are interested call me or come see me in the kiln room on Fridays from 8–9 a.m.	Ronny

As the time progressed and as the Original Five saw that more and more students were responding to and answering their posts, they decided to be a bit more daring and allow others to advertise on COOL-Bay. The following e-mail was sent to all students on campus.

To: Distribution List—ALL OEAFA Students
From: Ronny Teal
Date: February 1
Re: COOL-Bay

Hey,
There's a new site for all students at OEAFA. It's called COOL-Bay, and anyone can buy or sell anything on this site, and I MEAN ANYTHING!!!! Contact me if you are interested in being invited to this site, and you'll get private access to things you didn't know you needed or wanted. If you want to be a seller, just e-mail me what you want to sell with your contact info.

Peace.
COOL-Bay

This "COOL-Bay" was not a new site; it had been started during the first year that OEAFA was in operation. In fact, Ronny was the "inventor," as he liked to refer to himself, of COOL-Bay. Anyone who wanted to advertise anything on COOL-Bay had to get permission from Ronny before doing so, and he would review all possible posts, send them to the other Original Five to review and approve, then post them. Because the site was so popular and because students were really getting the hang of buying and selling things on COOL-Bay, the Original Five decided to get a bit bolder in what they advertised. Therefore, they approved to post the following to their COOL-Bay site.

Selling and Buying	Contact
Have you heard? It's easy to get what you want out of life. You just need to know how to manipulate people. It takes skill— So if you want to learn how to take what should be yours, contact me.	RSVP at 548-3359—key word: SexyHot You must have $20 ready in order to be admitted and another $20 to learn some new skills.
Want to impress your boyfriend? Then come to my house to learn how to please your man the way he wants to be pleased. We will teach you the best moves make you so desirable that any guy you meet will want you.	RSVP at 265-1151 $20 for admittance $20 for learning the skills $50 if you want to record your skill

Selling and Buying	*Contact*
Are you brave enough? Take risks and defy society's rules! Make your own life! If you are ready to show how brave you are then be ready and bring a gun or knife. There will be challenges with winners and losers. Which are you?	RSVP at 697-4488—key word: Brave— You'll be given directions on where to meet. $20 for admittance $1,000 for the bravest to be given at the end of the night

The Original Five were so surprised when the students from OEAFA were calling and actually paying to learn the different things being advertised. This was not your run of the mill selling and buying site: This was a student-driven site that was becoming a more clandestine, provocative moneymaker. What was even more fascinating was that students from other schools were told about COOL-Bay and wanted get in on the clandestine fun. However, as only OEAFA had access to the Student Café, the Original Five decided to create a website that would be an extension of the OEAFA COOL-Bay. This site's URL was e-mailed and texted to all known e-mail addresses of students who went to school in the Bortzview community and who attended OEAFA. This increase in popularity made COOL-Bay the place to find out where the best parties, drugs, sex, and alcohol were located. It was the hottest thing online, and it surely brought in some fast money to anyone who sold goods. This led the Original Five to think that they were invincible and indestructible, so they decided to post the following on both the OEAFA COOL-Bay Student Café and on the COOL-Bay website on the Internet.

A follow-up e-mail was sent to all e-mails that the Original Five had access to:

To: Distribution List—ALL OEAFA Students; Distribution List—ALL OEAFA Staff; Distribution List—EMAILS to Bortzview Students
From: Ronny Teal
Date: February 1
Re: New Post

Check out the new post on the COOL-Bay. You'll just die after reading it—or someone will! Click here to see the post on our website too. http:wlw.COOL-Bayoeafa.com

However, because Ronny was rushed due to using a school computer, he accidently invited every person who went to school outside of OEAFA and every person at OEAFA, including all OEAFA staff. Neither Ronny nor the Original Five knew that this occurred at first, but they quickly found out within five minutes of the e-mail's being sent.

What Just Happened?

Mrs. Lidia Limbaugh, an English teacher, rushed into Mr. Scheurich's office and showed him the e-mail invitation to Ronny's Student Café—COOL-Bay. She was not sure what she was reading because there were no blatant words that pointed to any violation of the school rules, so she thought. She knew, however, that it could not be good and did not know what this could mean for this online academy. So much time, effort, and money were spent on making this online school work, and now she was afraid that this one e-mail might ruin everything that everyone in this building worked so hard to make excellent. Just then, Dr. Laurent and Mr. Ted Walker, a history teacher, barged into Mr. Sheurich's office because they both just saw the e-mail moments before.

Dr. Laurent, like the others, was worried, yet confused because she, too, did not know exactly what she was looking at. Was it a plot for murder? Was it a terrorist threat? Or was it just fantasy. As she pondered aloud, more teachers rushed in with horror on their faces. She knew that this posting was much more than just a harmless prank. Because they have never had to deal with any real discipline problems, they were all at a loss of how to proceed with disciplining the students. Together, they came up with a plan:

1 All OEAFA staff would meet for an emergency meeting to occur in the next hour.
2 The computer techs would disable any student access to getting online for at least the end of the day and save all correspondence that has been gathered in the Student Café—COOL-Bay.
3 Dr. Laurent and Mr. Scheurich would contact Ronny and have him come into the office. Mr. Scheurich will have him write a statement and question him about the Student Café—COOL-Bay, as his name was on the e-mail.
4 Contact the superintendent and the school district chief of police.
5 Prepare a letter to be e-mailed to all OEAFA parents and students.

One of the teachers pointed out that other e-mail addresses, those from other schools in Bortzview, were also e-mailed. Dr. Laurent felt sick and realized that the students from other high schools within Bortview were contacted with this COOL-Bay e-mail, which definitely made the problem much bigger.

Dr. Laurent called in the technicians and asked, "How could this happen?" She wanted to know what type of firewalls were up and what else should have been done to prevented this. Questions about how and why the three techs did not catch this COOL-Bay site before it got so out of hand were asked, and questions about what else had not been caught became a huge worry.

After looking at the COOL-Bay Student Café area, the techs and Mr. Scheurich found that the COOL-Bay Student Café area had been created during the first year of the online school. He also relayed that there were many more provocative posts that eluded to illicit behavior that were posted during the short existence of the school. Dr. Laurent just shook her head in disbelief because she thought things were going so well for the Online Estes Fine Arts Academy. Why did she not know? What could she have done to prevent this? What more would be uncovered throughout the investigation? All these questions would need to wait, because she and Mr. Scheurich would need to prepare to talk to the staff.

WHAT ELSE DO I NEED TO KNOW?

The following is a brief insight into the issues presented in the case study, with a brief literature review to help give context to those issues.

Online Schools

Online learning is a type of education that can be found at the higher education level, and it is being seen more and more at the public education level. Students who may not be as successful in the traditional delivery of instruction, in a classroom with one teacher and thirty other students, may do very well with online learning. This type of instructional delivery has allowed parents and students to have a choice in education and has permitted students to learn at their own pace, at their own level, and using individualized curriculum. Most students who attend online schools are gifted students looking to work at their own pace; are prodigies in the areas of fine arts or athletics; need flexible hours for schooling and practice or training; are able to customize their learning; or do not feel safe at a brick-and-mortar school (Butler, 2010; Marsh, Carr-Chellman, & Sockman, 2009; Cavanagh, 2013).

Due to the successes of those students who are using online learning as an option for schooling, many public school districts have sought to create and include an online school as a choice for students within their district. In some school districts, these online schools are charters or are alternative specialized schools. Some charters are entities of school districts, while others are owned independently; regardless, they must comply with state requirements or charter agreements (Butler, 2010). Online learning is becoming so attractive because it allows for "individualized education plans, home school alternative, remedial option, innovative partnerships with universities, hospitals, etc., and returning students (i.e., dropouts who want to earn a GED)" (Butler, 2010, p. 46).

In the literature, online schools have different names or terms. Huerta, d'Entremont, and Gonzalez (2006) wrote how "cyber charters" have become popular and competitive to traditional brick-and-mortar schools due to some pointed characteristics:

1 Learning occurs primarily outside of a classroom and often in isolation from peers.
2 Instruction is delivered through an alternative medium.
3 Schools enroll students who did not previously attend public schools, especially home-schoolers.
4 Schools…can draw students from across a given state. (p. 24)

Waters, Barbour, and Menchaca (2014) have definitions for online learning, virtual schooling, and cyber schooling:

> … online learning refers to the practice of online learning for elementary and secondary students. Virtual school… refers to supplemental programs … offered online, taken by students who want to or need to supplement their course options. The term cyber school … refers to a publicly funded, full-time school. (p. 279)

Additionally, the virtual school usually serves students who are not successful in a brick-and-mortar, or traditional, type of school. They may have attendance issues, may have a disability, or may participate in Olympic-level sports (Marsh, Carr-Chellman, & Sockman, 2009). It should be noted that online learning is not a new phenomenon because distance learning has been in practice for many years; it refers to a "generic, all-inclusive term used to refer to the physical separation of teachers and learners" (as cited in Waters et al., 2014, p. 279). Some even employ a hybrid model, some are akin to homeschooling, and some are fully online, with no F2F contact.

The pluses toward online learning and why it is becoming such a popular choice for students and parents can be answered in the Marsh et al. (2009) research. They found that parents chose online charter schooling for their child because "technology can afford far greater attention to the individual needs of their children, more power, significant academic rigor, and a way to express their values within the traditional school curriculum" (p. 36). Furthermore, online learning is convenient for students, specifically for students who may have a part-time or full-time job, have children, or need an alternative way of getting a high school diploma. As learning can take place anywhere other than the school building, it makes learning more accessible and appealing. In fact, according to Shoaf's (2007) research, online learning allows for:

1 individualizing instruction,
2 pacing of instruction,
3 instruction in special subjects,
4 limitation of social engagement,
5 ability to modify lessons, and
6 organization of the school day. (p. 190)

Another great variable of online schools is that teachers are empowered because they get to be a part of setting up the learning platform and have a voice in how instruction will look online. This type of teaching is very time consuming at the beginning, but after a classroom is set up, tweaking it is easier. Schools that empower teachers making them a part of the decision making, improve the school climate, and decrease teacher turnover (Kahlenberg & Potter, 2015). In schools with greater teacher voice, the rates of conflict among teachers, administrators, and students also decrease. When the teachers are happy, the school climate and culture will be happier. When teachers are taken care of and are supported by administration, students, and parents, the school will function more smoothly, and both teachers and students will be successful.

One challenge with online education is that there is little research, so to affirm that student achievement will be better can be supported only if individual schools or school districts have determined that their online school is effective based on student success in grasping the curriculum goals and objectives. Furthermore, understanding which type of student would benefit most from online learning is not known through research at this time. Brady, Umpstead, and Eckes (2010) noted that online learning, or cyber charter schools, have raised concerns about the quality of education given to students when no F2F instruction is given. Additionally, they warned that "Cyber charter schools are relatively new and emerging as a type of alternative school. Since their creation, cyber charter schools have experienced a steady growth in number and geographic scope across the United States" (p. 191).

They continued by highlighting that several legal issues have arisen due to online schooling, which does not help the reputation of cyber schools or any online school. Additionally, some online schools are not accredited. Accreditation becomes a concern when students try to enroll in a public school after attending an online or virtual school but also when a student tries to enroll in college courses.

Finally, some parents are seeking online schooling because they believe that there is less threat of danger to occur. Specifically, crimes against persons are eliminated because online students do not have direct, physical contact with other persons. The parents believe that bullying, "mean girls," and social status issues are eliminated due to F2F's being eliminated but, as this case study has illuminated, one must ask, "Is online learning truly a safer place for students than a brick-and-mortar school?"

A School-within-a-School

Two schools sharing a single campus, with one as the main school and the other as the secondary school, is a common arrangement that is often referred to as a school-within-a-school. A school district might choose to locate two schools on one campus for a variety of reasons:

- The district has more identified schools that it has campuses, so some schools must double up and occupy one campus;
- housing two schools on a single campus might have economic advantages for the district over building a new school;
- two schools that have the same academic or disciplinary function— such as the disciplinary alternative education programs for both the middle school and the high school—can more easily and economically share resources if they are on the same campus; and
- when a campus is bigger than necessary for one school, a small charter or magnet school could fill the extra space.

The school-within-a-school plan can also be used to accommodate different teaching teams or to create distinct organizational areas that students and teachers are assigned to. For example, some high schools are divided into houses, families, or teams, with one principal leading the entire campus and assistant principal heading up each house, family, or team. The smaller schools might resemble this example:

- House 1—All freshman students and all freshman core classes are located in wing A.
- House 2—All sophomore students and all sophomore core classes are located in wing B.

Or this one:

- Blue Family—All freshmen, sophomores, juniors, and seniors who are assigned to the Blue Family will attend all their core courses in the Blue Hall. All electives will be located in the Green Hall.
- Yellow Family—All freshmen, sophomores, juniors, and seniors who are assigned to the Yellow Family will attend all their core courses in the Yellow Hall. All electives will be located in the Green Hall.

Regardless of the way a school-within-a-school is organized, the concept encourages the notion of a small school where students feel as if they are not just faces in the crowd but unique individuals who matter within their house, family, or team.

Schools-within-schools can also be specialized entities that have a particular focus and are available at all or some campuses, such as AVID (achievement via individual determination), IB (international baccalaureate), the Academy of Science, the Academy of Literature and the Arts, the Academy of the Fine Arts, the Academy of Leadership and Civics, the Academy of Community Service, the Academy School of Public Relations, or Junior Reserve Officers' Training Corps (JROTC). Like prospective OEAFA students, students who desire to attend these specialized schools may face a multifaceted application process with elements such as a series of interviews, an essay, a presentation of the essay or an audition before a panel of educators and peers, and recommendation letters from previous teachers. The rigorous curriculum of some of these campuses prepares students to attend military academies and Ivy League universities.

NCZ—NO CONSEQUENCE ZONE

Answer the questions below by applying what you know about this case and thinking about the steps you would take if you were faced with this situation or a similar one.

1 Providing a non-traditional type of schools is a good idea because it can reduce the drop-out rate for a school and district. Through online schooling, students are able to have flexible schedules to learn, work, and live.
   a. What type of non-traditional or alternative learning does your school district provide?
   b. Does your school district offer an online school? Is it successful, and how do you know?
   c. If your district does not have an online school, why not? What are the pros and cons of an online school for your students?
2 Students can break rules on campus or off campus, which is why many schools have contemplated or implemented an Honor Code.
   a. Does an Honor Code help students follow the rules? Why or why not?
   b. With an online school, does it make it easier for students to break rules and defy expectations more so than students at a brick-and-mortar school?
   c. How are rules enforced at a brick-and-mortar school? How should rules be enforced at an online school? Is there a difference?

3 Taking everything into account learned through this case study,
   a. How would the rules imposed in the school-within-a-school affect the main campus?
   b. What kinds of expectations should be decided upon when implementing a school-within-a-school?
4 Looking at the big picture,
   a. What are the social and financial implications of allowing the online school to continue?
   b. For the parents of OEAFA, what exactly should be said in the e-mail that Dr. Laurent and Mr. Scheurich will send?
   c. How might this same case study play out differently in your own community?

REFERENCES

Brady, K. P., Umpstead, R. R., & Eckes, S. (2010). Unchartered territory: The current legal landscape of public cyber charter schools. *Brigham Young University Education & Law Journal*, 2, 191–273.

Butler, K. (2010). Logging on to learn. *District Administration*, 46(3), 43–48.

Cavanagh, S. (2013). Urban districts creating virtual schools. *Education Week*, 32(33), 12–13.

Huerta, L., d'Entremont, C., & Gonzalez, M. (2006). Cyber charter schools: Can accountability keep pace with innovation? *Phi Delta Kappan*, 88(1), 23–30.

Kahlenberg, R., & Potter, H. (2015). Smarter charters. *Educational Leadership*, 72(5), 22–28.

Marsh, R., Carr-Chellman, A., & Sockman, B. (2009). Selecting silicon: Why parents choose cybercharter schools. *TechTrends*, 53(4), 32–36.

Shoaf, L. (2007). Perceived advantages and disadvantages of an online charter school. *American Journal of Distance Education*, 21(4), 185–198.

Waters, L. H., Barbour, M. K., & Menchaca, M. P. (2014). The nature of online charter schools: Evolution and emerging concerns. *Journal of Educational Technology & Society*, 17(4), 379–389.

Chapter 7

Bullies and Cyberbullies

Problems related to bullying via electronic devices are becoming more common and more visible on campuses. Some students use computers or personal devices during their free time at home to bully teachers and administrators and students on a campus. Is this type of "private" bullying by students allowed? Some students and parents in the following case study apparently believe that the answer to that question is yes, but where does harmless venting end and hurtful bullying begin?

This case study also considers the bullying of educators by parents, the flipped classroom, and the relationship between military installations and public school districts.

THE CASE

This year the educators at Truman Avenue High School (TAHS) introduced a new approach regarding students bringing their personal electronic devices to school. With the approval of the school board, the TAHS Academic Committee—made up of administrators, teachers, and students—added the following policy to the Student Code of Conduct (SCOC) and the student handbook:

> Each student is encouraged to bring to school an electronic tablet, computer notebook, phone with Internet capabilities, or other personal electronic device with Internet capabilities, for the sole purpose of using the device as an instructional aid. All students and their parents must submit documentation (TAHS Electronic Device Policy Form) showing that they understand the rules of having and using an electronic device on campus for learning and that they

understand the consequences if this privilege is abused. Consequences for the inappropriate use of an electronic device can include revocation of the privilege of bringing electronic devices to school, in-school suspension, out-of-school suspension, or any other disciplinary measure that aligns with the Student Code of Conduct.

Many teachers and students were enthusiastic about this policy change because now students would have easier access to the Internet for research, could use various kinds of digital learning applications, and would be more motivated to pay attention in class. The administrators and many parents were uneasy, however. They worried that expensive electronic devices (EDs) might be stolen, that some parents could not afford to equip their children with EDs for school, and that SCOC violations might increase. In any case, the new policy was in effect, and its ramifications would soon be known. The policy's proponents suggested that the best defense against SCOC violations would be to continuously remind students and parents of the consequences involved.

An unfortunate reality was that no professional development course was provided for teachers on how to use the types of EDs that their students would be bringing to class. Some teachers were motivated enough to search the Web to find apps that would enhance classroom instruction and student learning. Those who had no desire or motivation to use the EDs without first receiving a professional development course about them decided not to incorporate EDs into their lesson plans. The TAHS administrators supported the teachers in making their own decisions and asked the central office to offer professional development courses throughout the school year on how to use EDs as instructional tools in the classroom.

Captain and Mrs. Jordan

Mrs. Jordan started her teaching career in another state, but because her husband's army career has meant frequent moves, she has taught English classes in five different Department of Defense schools within the ten years that she has been teaching. She was pleased to come to TAHS a year ago, because teaching at a public school would be a change of pace for her. She embraced the opportunity to work with both the nonmilitary students and families who live in Truman's attendance zone and local military students and families who are associated with her husband's battalion. She has always felt an especially strong connection with the families she sees, not only at school but at military functions.

Now in her second year at Truman, Mrs. Jordan is excited about the school district's new policy on EDs. She feels confident about incorporating the Internet and other computer devices into her teaching methods, and she already knows which educational apps she will use to help her students to grasp the English curriculum. She was excited to flip her classroom and apply the tenets of the flipped classroom to all the courses she teaches. The flipped classroom would allow so much more student-directed learning during class time, which would help them to understand concepts quicker and, hopefully, enjoy English more.

Her husband, Captain Jordan, is in an engineer battalion, and both his executive officer, Major Laurel, and his battalion commander, Colonel Oliver, have children enrolled at TAHS. In fact, the colonel's son Ty and post commander General Ames's son Chris are best friends and are in Mrs. Jordan's sophomore English class this year.

Captain and Mrs. Jordan are the epitome of a military couple: He is a graduate of United States Military Academy, and she volunteers every chance she gets. The captain was first in his class at West Point, and his dedication to the military is evident in his Officer Evaluation Reports, which have always given him a rating of "1," or excellent. Additionally, he recently made the recommendation list for promotion to major, ensuring that he will have a long career in the military. It is even rumored that Captain Jordan will be a general one day, because of his and his wife's commitment to the army.

The Digital Debacle

As the school year progressed, only a few minor issues arose involving student use of electronic devices in the classroom, and the two thefts that were reported were quickly solved when lockers were searched. Overall, the teachers were happy with the new policy on EDs. Mrs. Jordan was one teacher who was having great success with having her students use their EDs as instructional tools. In general, her students followed her lead and respected her classroom rules.

She changed all her classes to flipped classes, which meant that she created videos of her lecturing and different images of topics that students were learning for a given week and uploaded those to a shared site for the students to access. Then, during class, she made sure that the students were involved with application-based activities to ensure that the students could practice what they studied the night before. For example, during the unit on literary elements, Mrs. Jordan created several videos that showed the different literary elements that could be found in literature. She also created an electronic binder with handouts, skills lessons, and short stories that her students could access at home to prepare for the next day. During class time, students worked collaboratively on group activities that focused on the videos and learning that happened the night before. This flipped idea was really working for her students, and she was so excited to see her students become successful in their learning.

However, Mrs. Jordan did notice that Ty and Chris were being more talkative in class, and they sometimes disregarded her established rules: specifically when they were using their EDs. In one incident, the two boys were sitting in the back of the room, talking and laughing about something they were both viewing on Ty's tablet. As Mrs. Jordan was teaching, she asked the boys to put their EDs away and listen to her lecture. They openly ignored her and continued laughing and talking aloud. Mrs. Jordan finished her lesson, directed the other students to start their group work, and then walked over to Ty and Chris. She asked them to step into the hallway with her, and they did. As she started to say something to them, Ty blurted out, "Later, Mrs. Jordan." Chris added, "You know we make our own rules!" Mrs. Jordan was stunned into silence as she watched them walk down the hallway and out the doors toward their cars.

Mrs. Jordan reported the boys to the truancy officer for leaving class without permission, and she notified their parents, making contact with their mothers. The boys were unhappy that their parents had been called, and they skipped the next two days of school, avoiding Mrs. Jordan's class. In fact, they were misbehaving in other classes they had together, and they chose to skip all classes to avoid getting into trouble in them, too.

When the boys came back to school, Mrs. Jordan's class was working on creating literature books, using an educational app. Mrs. Jordan sat down with Ty and Chris as the other students worked and explained the rubric for constructing their books. As she was explaining, Chris stood up and hollered, "This is bullshit! I don't have time for this elementary shit!" Ty chimed in, "Come on, Chris. Let's get out of here!" Both boys packed up their things and began to walk out of the classroom. Mrs. Jordan asked them to stop, and they retorted, "Go f—— yourself," as Ty grabbed his crouch and Chris gestured with his finger. At this, a shaken Mrs. Jordan directed her other students to continue working on their books. After class, she walked down to the assistant principal's office and wrote discipline referrals for Ty and Chris. Then she called their parents to let them know what had occurred during class. She was able to get ahold of the boys' mothers, who were mortified once again and thanked Mrs. Jordan for the information. They also apologized profusely for their sons' actions.

At the end of the day, Mrs. Jordan was finishing up some paperwork in her classroom when General Ames walked in. Immediately, she noticed that he was very upset, and she was startled by his loud and forceful voice. She also noticed that he was not wearing the required nametag, which meant he had not checked in with the front office staff. He bluntly told her that his wife had called him about Chris and that he did not appreciate being bothered at work for something that a teacher should be able to handle. He continued belittling Mrs. Jordan, telling her that she obviously did not have the guts to call him and that was why she had called his wife. He finished by demanding that she rescind Chris's discipline referral and saying that if she had any future problems with Chris, she should "fuc!#@" deal with them herself and not bother his wife or him again. At that, he turned and walked out without giving Mrs. Jordan a chance to respond.

Mrs. Jordan did not rescind Chris's and Ty's discipline referrals and, despite General Ames's intimidation tactics, she did report the incident with him to the assistant principals (APs). Because Ty and Chris had skipped class, been insubordinate, and used profanity, the APs suspended both boys for three days, and citations (summons) were given for disruption of the educational environment. They also reminded Mrs. Jordan that she could file charges with the school resource officer against General Ames for using profanity and disrupting the educational environment, but she declined. Mrs. Jordan thought that the school's discipline of the boys would be enough. It is possible General Ames violated the trespassing statutes by not signing in at the front office and proceeding into an area reserved for those with implied permission (students, teachers, school employees, and those who have signed in and received permission to proceed).

Later that night, Mrs. Jordan told her husband about the day's events but, before she could finish, he told her he already knew, because Colonel Oliver called him into his office. The colonel said that Captain Jordan needed to talk to his wife about her lack of respect for families with higher rank and that his son Ty was a good boy and could not have done the things Mrs. Jordan had accused him of. Captain Jordan, who did not know why he was being told this information, replied, "My wife is an exceptional educator, and I support her one hundred percent in the decisions she makes on her campus and in her classroom. I don't question her decisions, just as she does not question the decisions I make on my job." However, that was not what the colonel wanted to hear. He told the captain, "Looks like you may have a shorter military career than we thought."

The next morning, Mrs. Jordan decided to withdraw the boys' referrals after all because she and her husband worked so hard as a military couple to earn rank and do well. Never before had they encountered superiors who behaved as the general and the colonel had, and never before had they been bullied and threatened by superiors. She hoped that if she rescinded the referrals, her husband might have an easier time at work.

However, when Mrs. Jordan walked into the APs' office, the APs told her that they had received a tip that Ty and Chris had created a website depicting Mrs. Jordan as a porn star. They had cut and pasted her school picture onto photos of naked women who were doing X-rated sexual acts online. Ty and Chris had texted the website's link to students throughout the campus and had also tweeted and Instagamed the link. The APs wanted Mrs. Jordan to be prepared for questions from students throughout the day, and they offered her the option of going home.

Mrs. Jordan was devastated. She sat down to catch her breath. After a few moments, she stated firmly, "I'm not going anywhere. I did nothing wrong, and as long as you are planning to severely punish them according to the SCOC, I will go teach my classes." The APs promised that they would hand out the SCOC's harshest punishments to the boys.

As Mrs. Jordan walked to her classroom, she heard students whispering, "She got hers!" and "She shouldn't have messed with them!" She even heard the words "slut" and "whore." Distraught, she made it to her classroom and called her husband. Maybe it was time for them to make another army move.

WHAT ELSE DO I NEED TO KNOW?

The following is a brief insight into the issues presented in the case study, with a brief literature review to help give context to those issues.

Electronic Devices in the Classroom

Electronic devices and social media, such as Facebook and Twitter, are seemingly ubiquitous and can easily become channels for SCOC or penal code violations when they contain words or pictures that are inappropriate, demeaning, or threatening to others. Additionally, educators need to be aware that some savvy students may torment or retaliate against others by creating a webpage or pages and/or posting tweets that are slanderous or humiliating and are used to bully their targets into submission. Stopping student cyberbullies may seem impossible, especially when they create their propaganda at home and avoid bringing it into the educational environment.

When it comes to using EDs as an instructional tool on campuses, reviews from educators are mixed. For some educators, having EDs in the classroom can be a very good thing. In fact, more and more schools are allowing EDs to be used in the classroom because of the benefits that contribute to student success (Criswell, 2009; Khadaroo, 2012; Foote, 2012; Sun, Martinez, & Seli, 2014). At a high school in Austin, Texas, a librarian implemented the use of iPads and encouraged teachers to start using iPads in the classroom (Foote, 2012). As the teachers began to use the iPads, they found that their students were having fun learning and performing beyond expectations. The use of different educational apps on the iPads allowed the educators to "...facilitate access to information, help kids learn, and empower them" (Foote, p. 33).

The use of technology can make learning accessible from any place. As Kennedy (2012) stated, "Computer-powered devices are making anytime, anywhere learning a reality. They make it easier for learning to continue and be reinforced outside the school walls" (p. 34–35). Better classroom experiences start with electronic devices because students are able to collaborate on projects and discussion groups that promote more student-driven learning (Raths, 2013). Additionally, students are more creative when they are given the opportunity to use an electronic device and produce a learning product that is not a mobile, poster, or other antiquated medium.

Many educators use EDs in the classroom and have found online communities that serve as support groups in promoting technology in the classroom. Educators can join other educators who use EDs and share in the learning of how those devices can promote successful learning annually during the National Digital Learning Day. This day is set aside for educators to "showcase how technology can improve student outcomes and support teachers," as Bob Wise, president of the Alliance for Excellent Education stated (as cited in Alliance for Excellent Education, 2014).

In contrast, there are issues that some find to outweigh the benefits of allowing EDs in schools. Two regular issues pertain to cost and property management, where a school may need to purchase EDs to ensure equal access to students who may not have the personal capital to purchase an ED (Criswell, 2009). This extra money for purchase does not always include the maintenance or replacement of lost, damaged, or stolen EDs. Additionally, although allowing electronic devices in the classroom is innovative and encourages creativity, there are serious problems that come with this privilege. According to Nworie and Haughton (2008), some problems include

> technology supported cheating opportunities; communication-related distractions from emails, instant messaging, computer games, web surfing, and other 'personal projects'; lack of engagement ...; and lately, increasing incidents of bullying and intimidation supported with innovations including the Internet, text messaging, and social network sites. (p. 52)

These problems place even more pressure on educators as they try to encourage student success.

Another issue that EDs bring to the classroom is that it is a recording device. Honawar (2008) found that cell phone use in the classroom has increased the number of videos that students record of teachers singing, dancing, or doing something that will land on the Internet. This fear of recording has affected some students not to participate in class for fear of saying or doing something that will be mocked online. The recording could be elaborated in a webpage designed specifically for the purpose to harm another person. When this happens, defamation could be a result and will deter a successful learning environment for all students.

There must be policies in place that point to the proper and improper use of EDs that are clear and understandable by both students and parents

(Quillen, 2010). A campus-wide policy or classroom expectations on the use of EDs in the school is necessary, as teachers' and students' perceptions of the appropriate use of EDs differ (Baker, Lusk, & Neuhauser, 2012). Students and parents must understand what advantages an ED may involve and the consequences of neglecting to adhere to the policy.

Hence, many districts have implemented guidelines for ED use on campuses. For example:

Rules for the Use of Electronic Devices on Campus
All professional staff using electronic devices (EDs) in the classroom will take these actions:

- participate in professional development courses throughout the school year that focus on the best ways to implement EDs in classroom instruction;
- show and note how EDs will be used when writing lesson plans;
- keep parents informed as to how EDs are being used to enhance instruction and what the benefits are and have been throughout the year;
- inform parents which apps are being used and provide instructions and/or parent class nights on how to use them;
- share ideas and lessons during team learning time, faculty meetings, and professional development sessions;
- enforce the rules and expectations for all when EDs are in use;
- have students and parents sign contracts that describe the classroom expectations and outline the consequences of not abiding by them; photocopies of this signed contract will be sent to the parents and to the assistant principals' office; if both a student and the student's parent refuse to sign, they forfeit the student's right to use EDs in the classroom for instructional purposes; and
- include students who do not have personal EDs available by providing them with school-issued EDs.

All students using EDs in the classroom will do the following:

- use the EDs for educational purposes *only* and not for personal reasons;
- abide by all school and classroom rules concerning EDs;
- if any bullying of others is done through an ED device or if any bullying material is forwarded that affects the learning environment negatively, the following consequences will be administered:
  - the student will be banned from using EDs on campus for a designated amount of time and
  - the student will be disciplined according to the SCOC, which may call for suspension, the issuance of a citation or summons, or a recommendation for placement in a disciplinary alternative education program.

School districts that allow students to use school-issued equipment must be able to keep track of not only the EDs but the websites visited. Many school districts enforce policies that give them access to both student and employee computers, and when a district finds that its policies have not been followed, they may reprimand the student or employee.

The Flipped Classroom

A flipped class is a delivery of instruction that can be easily implemented in a blended course because it combines online and F2F methods of learning (Jordan, 2012; Kennedy, 2012). It can involve uploading short videos focused on a specific topic to an online learning platform, while allowing F2F time for whole-/small-group discussions and guided practice (Bergmann, Overmyer, & Wilie, 2011). In essence, lecturing and direct teaching occurs online, on a student's own time, while the guided practice or facilitated learning occurs in the F2F classroom with the teacher present. The online learning allows the student to take time learning key concepts and revisiting a video again and again, as needed. It also allows F2F learning to be a time for immediate feedback to occur and questions to be answered in a timelier manner.

Flipping a classroom has many benefits and is ideal for any class since it is

- a means to INCREASE interaction and personalized contact time between students and teachers;
- an environment where students take responsibility for their own learning;
- a class where content is permanently archived for review or remediation; and
- a place where all students can get a personalized education.

(Bergmann et al., 2011, para 3)

Flipped classrooms are not places to substitute teaching with videos, and increase "extra" or "free" time in class (Spencer, Wolf, & Sams, 2011). It is not a tool that replaces effective teaching or time to focus on lower levels of learning, such as surface or declarative learning (Bain, 2004). Instead, flipping a class provides more focused time on student-centered learning.

The biggest benefits of a flipped classroom are the ability for students to learn not only from the teacher but from one another and to help the teacher to learn exactly where a student is excelling and struggling (Flipped Classroom Offers New Learning Path, 2011; Flipping Classrooms, 2011; Hart, 2012). Flipping does away with the need for teachers to spoon-feed students and allows for students to reach the highest levels of Bloom's, learning at their own pace. The F2F class time becomes a place of questioning, higher order thinking, critical thinking, and focused learning. An additional benefit, according to Kahn, from Kahn Academy, is that flipping "humanises" the learning experience for students by removing the 'one-size-fits-all' lecture from the classroom in favour of a 'self- paced' lecture at home" (as cited in Evans, 2011, p. 4). It allows for more interaction and the personalization of contact time between students and students, and students and teachers. Furthermore, as videos are found on an online platform, they can be archived and viewed again at a different time. This helps those students who missed a F2F class and those who are struggling with a concept (Evans, 2011).

Bullying of Educators

When one thinks about bullying, the image usually includes students bullying other students. However, bullying can occur between teacher and teacher, administrator and teacher, parent and teacher, parent and parent, student and student, student and teacher, and so on. Numerous types of situations could involve a bully, but educators must be aware that a bully could be anyone, and the bullied could be one person or several.

Most state educational and criminal codes recognize bullying between children but not between adults. If a parent bullies another adult on a campus, that behavior might be legally defined as a verbal assault, an assault, a terrorist threat, or retaliation. Parents do have the right to visit a school to talk to teachers, and many state educational and federal codes give parents the leeway to request almost anything. Ultimately, though, it is up to the educator to consider and fulfill or deny a request. Additionally, even a parent who is an army general or the top lawyer in a city cannot force an educator to do anything as long as the educator follows the school board's policies. Administrators must always support educators if a parent intimidates and threatens them for reporting such incidents according to the district's policies.

If an educator feels that the bullying has crossed over to defamation, a legal action may be pursued. "The law of civil defamation says, in effect, that one individual may not harm another's reputation by false statements about his or her character" (McDaniel, 2002, p. 34). Unfortunately, the Internet has made it easier for defamation to occur, and the laws that protect persons against Internet defamation are currently found at the state level. According to Taylor (2002), defamation is "deliberate, false, written or oral communication that injures a person's reputation" and is a problem that is common on school campuses (p. 67). Additionally,

> Written defamation is commonly referred to as libel, and spoken defamation is generally referred to as slander; but those plane distinctions are not always precise for legal purpose. It must be false, it must be published, and it must damage or injure a person's reputation, business, or profession. (Taylor, 2002, p. 67)

Defamation can occur when a parent talks about an educator in a false light to others or when students post fabrications and falsehoods on a webpage. Internet speech is protected under the First Amendment; however, if defamation can be proven to follow the definition above, a legal action may be taken.

Computers can also house pictures and videos that can be transmitted over several types of social media, such as Facebook, Instagram, The Vine, Kik, Yik Yak, and so on. Would there be liability in possessing or sending out these pictures and videos? Stewart (2013) discussed how the Internet has made it possible and easy for others to repost things that may be seen as defamatory by others. He pointed to the muddy waters that concern posting something on social media and others reposting that same information elsewhere. As there are many cases that point to social media defamation but not one clear case for schools to follow when disciplining students, it is best to seek clarification from the local school board.

Administrators should adhere to guidelines regarding bullying of their educators, such as the following:

- Teachers and other educators should be informed that they have the right to file a police report when they have been threatened, retaliated against, or assaulted by a parent, a student, or anyone else. Of course, they also have the right to file a police report when they have been the victim of any other type of penal code violation, such as the harassment statutes.
- Teachers and other educators should be introduced to and know how to contact the school resource officer or the law enforcement agency with competent jurisdiction, as needed, especially when a penal code or SCOC violation has occurred.
- Teachers and other educators should never be treated as if they deserved or brought any threatening, intimidating, or other inappropriate behavior from another person on themselves.

In an article that focuses on teacher-to-teacher bullying, the following abbreviated steps were offered to help control bullying from one person to another:

1 identify bullying behaviors,
2 stand up for others,
3 stop it at the source, and
4 document your experiences. (Anonymous, 2012, p. 69)

To foster an environment of safety and security, educators should work together as a family in protecting themselves and others on campus from verbal and physical assaults and retaliation for performing their job as the school board dictates.

The laws regarding EDs and bullying are changing regularly, so be diligent in keeping up with the current codes. Administrators must contend with ED use and bullying on campus and must establish and communicate clear expectations and guidelines for teachers, students, and parents. In addition, these expectations and guidelines must be administered uniformly throughout a campus and among all parties. Finally, administrators need to think about the implications of placing staff pictures on their school's website and other personal information, such as a biography that may include family pictures.

NCZ—NO CONSEQUENCE ZONE

Answer the questions below by applying what you know about this case and thinking about the steps you would take if you were faced with this situation or a similar one.

1 Bullying by students through the use of EDs is becoming more and more common.
   a. How does your school district's SCOC and your state's penal code protect educators and others from bullying students who create webpages designed to abuse and humiliate others?
   b. What elements does your SCOC or parent handbook contain that address the behaviors of parents, specifically using intimidation and profanity against a teacher or administrator? Do revisions need to be made to these documents to further protect the educators in your district?
2 Sometimes educators bring their home life to school, or vice versa.
   a. When a disruption occurs on campus that includes aspects of an educator's personal and professional life, what, if any, are the duties of the administration?
   b. Discuss examples of home-life and school-life issues. What are some ways to avoid mixing the two?
3 The SCOC should clearly outline the district's rules for students and the consequences for violating them. Administrators should ensure that the contents of the SCOC are consistently communicated to all stakeholders, with reminders throughout the year.
   a. According to your SCOC, what are the options for educators when students walk out of class or skip class?
   b. What are the options for educators when students use profanity in the classroom and disrupt the learning environment?
4 According to the rules stated in your SCOC, what types of consequences should Ty and Chris receive for their actions?

5 On many military installations, post or base commanders and battalion commanders encourage their troops to be positive influences in their children's lives. Additionally, the commanders often create partnerships with educators and encourage them to contact the officer in charge or the noncommissioned officer in charge when a troop member's child is not following school rules and policies and the troop member has not been cooperative in addressing the situation. Finally, if military personnel behave in a manner unbecoming of a military person, discipline may be imminent.

   a. Do students from military families attend schools in your district? If so, does a partnership exist between the local military installation and your school district, and how does it work?

   b. What types of partnerships have been created with the nonmilitary businesses in your community that encourage a positive relationship between students and educators?

6 Now consider some of the effects of bullying on the larger community.

   a. What are the social and political implications for the educators at TAHS if parents are allowed to intimidate teachers without reprimand?

   b. How might a situation like the one presented in this case study play out differently in your own community?

7 The delivery of instruction has changed throughout the years, and now flipping a classroom has become a popular way to deliver course concepts and objectives.

   a. Does your school have flipped classrooms? If so, what do they look like?

   b. What are pros and cons of a flipped classroom, and what type of policy or rules need to be in place for the flipped classroom to work?

   c. What are learning activities and applications that could be used in a flipped classroom?

REFERENCES

Alliance for Excellent Education. (2014). Digital learning day 2015 set for Friday, March 13. Retrieved from http://all4ed.org/press/digital-learning-day-2015-set-for-friday-march-13/

Anonymous. (2012). Call it what it is: Confronting the teacher-on-teacher bully down the hall. *English Journal*, 101(6), 64–69

Bain, K. (2004). *What the best college teachers do*. Boston, MA: President and Fellows of Harvard College.

Baker, W., Lusk, E., & Neuhauser, K. L. (2012). On the use of cell phones and other electronic devices in the classroom: Evidence from a survey of faculty and students. *Journal of Education for Business*, 87(5), 275–289.

Bergmann, J., Overmyer, J., & Wilie, B. (2011). The flipped class: What it is and what it is not. *The Daily Riff.* Retrieved from http://www.thedailyriff.com/articles/the-flipped-class-conversation-689.php

Criswell, C. (2009). The computer in your student's pocket. *Teaching Music,* 172, 10.

Evans, D. (2011). Turning lessons upside down. *The Times Educational Supplement,* (7) 4. Retrieved from http://search.proquest.com/docview/911106744?accountid= 27965

Flipped Classroom Offers New Learning Path. (2011). *Electronic Education Report,* 18(23), 1–3.

Flipping classrooms. (2011). *Phi Delta Kappan,* 93(4), 6.

Foote, C. (2012). iPads for everyone. *School Library Journal,* 48(10), 30–33.

Hart, M. (2012). A time and a place? *T H E Journal,* 39(4), 6.

Honawar, V. (2008). Cell phone in classrooms land teachers on online video sites. *Education Digest,* 73(6), 29–33.

Jordan, C. (2012). Flipped class method gaining ground. *District Administration,* 48(1), 64.

Kennedy, M. (2012). Left to their own devices. *American School and University,* 84(9), 34–37.

Khadaroo, S. T. (2012). Education 2.0: Can digital learning day begin a classroom revolution? *Christian Science Monitor,* http://www.csmonitor.com/USA/Education/2012/0201/Education-2.0-Can-Digital-Learning-Day-begin-a-classroom-revolution

McDaniel, T. R. (2002). Keeping defame from costing defortune. *The Education Digest,* 68(3), 34–37.

Nworie, J., & Haughton, N. (2008). Good intentions and unanticipated effects: The unintended consequences of the application of technology in teaching and learning environments. *TechTrends,* 52(5), 52–58.

Quillen, I. (2010). Framework crafted for student use of computing devices. *Education Week,* 30(11). Retrieved from http://www.edweek.org/ew/articles/2010/11/10/11devices.h30.html

Raths, D. (2013). Crossing the device divide. *T H E Journal,* 40(5), 9–13.

Spencer, D., Wolf, D., & Sams, A. (2011). Are you ready to flip? *The Daily Riff.* Retrieved from http://www.thedailyriff.com/articles/the-flipped-class-conversation-689.php

Stewart, D. R. (2013). When retweets attack: Are twitter users liable for republishing the defamatory tweets of others? *Journalism and Mass Communication Quarterly,* DOI:10.1177/1077699013482913

Sun, J. C.-Y., Martinez, B., & Seli, H. (2014). Just-in-time or plenty-of-time teaching? Different electronic feedback devices and their effect on student engagement. *Educational Technology & Society,* 17(2), 234–244.

Taylor, K. (2002). Sticks and stones: When words hurt the principal. *Principal Leadership,* 2(5), 67–70.

Chapter 8

The Dual-Language Pre-K Program

Teachers work with a diverse population of students, which means that they also work with a diverse population of parents. Teachers who work with students who are trying to learn a second language may meet even more diversity issues, specifically the biases of certain parents. In the following case, a dual-language pre-kindergarten classroom sets the stage for an irate parent to demand the unthinkable. Unfortunately, some parents have expectations that are not realistic or are discriminatory to other students and educators. In the following, one such parent is illustrated.

THE CASE

The Quintessential Pre-K Teacher

Mrs. Duran has been a pre-kindergarten (Pre-K) teacher for more than half her teaching career, and she still loves her job after thirty-three years in the classroom. She is an exceptional Pre-K teacher, one who is respected and adored by her colleagues at Mitchell Elementary. Each year, parents place their child's name on a waiting list to be placed in Mrs. Duran's classroom, because her reputation is sound, and she is revered in the small rural town of Arthur.

The City of Arthur has a population of nearly 7,000, and it has one stoplight, a Dairy Queen, a Dollar Store, and about 1,200 starter homes. The rest of the town of Arthur is made up of trailer homes and homes that have been in place since the early 1940s. And there are many residents who own ranches full of livestock, live in the county, and have an Arthur address. Arthur was incorporated ten years ago, and the city council has tried to ensure a great relationship with the Arthur schools, so together they can work at promoting the City of Arthur to encourage young families to move there and put their children through the school system. The Arthur School District has four schools: two elementary schools, one middle school, and one high school.

Mrs. Duran lives in a suburb about thirty minutes away from Arthur. She grew up in a metropolitan area and always lived in cities with populations of 100,000 or more. What attracted her to teach in Arthur was the small-town atmosphere that is very familial. She came to Arthur about twenty-three years ago and plans to retire in five years. She loves teaching young minds, and she is very excited about her new teaching responsibilities that include teaching in the new dual-language program, which she helped create. She and another teacher had co-taught both English and Spanish learners together throughout the entire last year in a 50/50 dual-language classroom through a pilot dual-language program. Due to their classroom success in helping both sets of learners become energized about learning English and Spanish while learning the Pre-K curriculum, the principal at Mitchell Elementary requested that Mitchell fully implement a full dual-language program for grades Pre-K through fifth grade.

Dual Language at Mitchell

Dr. Lupe Mins has been the principal of Mitchell Elementary for two years. As a new principal, she believes in the English/Spanish dual-language program (DLP) and was so thrilled to receive information from the Arthur School District that her campus would be the site of the DLP. The other elementary principal did not want the program and was happy that his campus was not considered, as he did not truly believe in students learning two languages. Therefore, all parents who wanted their children to be in the Pre-K DLP program would attend Mitchell Elementary, and all other students would attend a "regular" Pre-K at the other elementary.

The DLP was a new concept for Arthur Schools and one that followed state code. Because of the influx of Spanish-speaking families moving to the City of Arthur, the school had to provide a bilingual education to the Spanish-speaking students. The bilingual education could be through a DLP, which Arthur wanted to implement; therefore, much preparation during the pilot year (last year) took place. Several parents' nights were held for interested families to learn about the DLP, and a flier that highlighted the positives was mailed to every home with an Arthur address. The flier included the following:

Arthur Elementary is offering a Dual-Language Program (DLP) next school year! All students who qualify for the DLP will be a part of two classrooms:

- One English-only classroom with a certified English-as-a-second-language (ESL) teacher and
- one Spanish-only classroom with a certified bilingual teacher.

Our DLP will follow a 50/50 model, which means that students will learn English 50% of the time and Spanish 50% of the time in all core subjects (English/language arts, math, science, and social studies)

A commitment of six years is needed from you and your child. Your child will start in pre-kindergarten and will exit from the DLP after his/her fifth grade year.

After six years in our DLP, your child will become PROFICIENT in English and Spanish when

- writing,
- speaking, and
- reading.

All students interested in the DLP must go through a series of assessments in the academic, emotional, and behavioral areas.

Come to our first parent night where more information will be shared about this great opportunity for your child.

In addition, parents were told that the DLP would be implemented starting with the Pre-K and kindergarten grades and that each year a new grade would be added until all grades from Pre-K through fifth grade would have a DLP bilingual/ESL team. Many parents were very excited about having their child learn two languages, and they attended every meeting and prepared to sign contracts that dedicated their child to six years in the DLP.

In addition to the meetings, each prospective student had to be assessed to ensure they were academically, emotionally, and behaviorally prepared to enter in a program that would be very rigorous and fast-paced. Either a bilingual or an ESL teacher would assess each student with a series of questions, first in the student's native language and then in the second language. The order of the assessment questions followed the partial guidelines seen below.

Assessment

Academic

1 Ask each student the following and wait for a verbal response.
- Tell me your name and spell your name.
- Recite the alphabet.
- Tell me your home address.
- Count to the highest number you know.

- Tell me about your favorite time of year and explain what makes it so special.

2 Have students read aloud the following sight words:
- run
- walk
- name
- happy
- play
- house
- go
- it
- to
- stop

3 Have the students write
- their name
- as many letters as possible, in order
- as many numbers as possible, in order
- words that they may know, in either their native or second language

4 Have students read the given passage and ask a series of questions, such as
- What happened in the story?
- Who were the characters in the story?
- What happened at the beginning of the story?
- What was the most exciting or saddest part of the story?
- What would you have done differently if you were the main character?

5 Have students draw a series of pictures and shapes, which include a
- circle
- square
- triangle
- house
- dog
- bus
- car
- best friend
- family

6 For the emotional and behavioral portion of the assessment, check all the emotions and behaviors observed throughout the assessment by completing the checklist below.

Emotional—Circle the emotion observed.

- Student seemed *happy—sad—unemotional—scared—worried—eager* when he/she entered the assessment room.

- Student seemed *happy—sad—unemotional—scared—worried—eager* while completing the verbal portion of the assessment.

- Student seemed *happy—sad—unemotional—scared—worried—eager* while completing the written portion of the assessment.

- Student seemed *happy—sad—unemotional—scared—worried—eager* while completing the reading portion of the assessment.

- Student seemed *happy—sad—unemotional—scared—worried—eager* while completing the drawing portion of the assessment.

- Student seemed *happy—sad—unemotional—scared—worried—eager* when he/she left the assessment room.

Behavioral—Circle the behavior observed. If you must redirect the student, tally the number of times the redirection occurred.

- Student *sat—stood most—some—none* of the time while completing each activity. The student had to be redirected ___ times.

- Student *waited—did not wait* for teacher to finish asking each question before answering *most—some—none* of the time. The student had to be redirected ___ times.

As the DLP would start its implementation at the Pre-K and kindergarten levels, Mrs. Mins wanted one bilingual teacher and one ESL teacher to be paired as a team. Between the two, the teachers would share forty students, with about twenty students speaking English as their first language and about twenty students speaking Spanish as their first language. Hence, the bilingual teacher would have twenty mixed Spanish- and English-speaking students in her class while the ESL teacher would have the other twenty mixed Spanish- and English-speaking students. Pre-K would have one set of DLP teachers, and Kindergarten would have two sets of DLP teachers, due to the demand of the program. All DLP teachers were sent to professional development on how to team-teach students who would essentially be learning a full year of curriculum in half the time. Essentially, a school year consists of about 187 days of instruction, which the DLP would need to teach in about 93 days.

Each day, both teams would teach the same lesson. For example, if the bilingual teacher taught the students about the color red and the letters "A" and "S," the ESL teacher would teach exactly the same lesson in English. The next day, the teamed teachers would switch students and teach the exact lesson to the new set of students in the other language. If one walked into the bilingual teacher's classroom, the centers, word wall, games, songs, and the like would all be in Spanish, where the opposite would be found in English in the ESL room. The saturation of both languages would help each student learn the languages easily.

There was some dissension from some parents and teachers, however, on what language should be taught, how the DLP should be run, and how the money needed for start-up would be spent. Some felt that English should be the only language taught until middle grades, while others felt that the *"illegal immigrants"* were *"stealing our kids money!"* and did not want their tax money spent on anything other than their own children. To implement a successful DLP, about $100,000 was spent to cover Spanish and English books for the library, furniture, rugs, games, and a curriculum that was geared toward the 50/50 model of dual-language and that aligned to the state standards. For a small school district with limited funds, this was a lot of money. Although the bilingual funds would be used to buy most of the items, money from the campus instructional fund would need to be used to cover the rest of the cost. This realization did not sit well with parents and teachers who felt that Arthur was a poor school district and barely had enough money to cover the costs of the general education program.

Dr. Mins did not want any student or family to feel as if English was being replaced by Spanish, nor did she want anyone to feel that money was being misspent inappropriately on a fly-by-night program, so she took much effort in answering questions and concerns that had anything to do with the DLP. She also took time to point out not only the benefits that the Spanish-speaking students would gain but the benefits the English-speaking students would gain (e.g., acquiring a second language proficiently could lead students learning a third language in middle or high school, making the students very marketable for the job market). Dr. Mins' efforts paid off, and a great number of parents wanted their children to be a part of the DLP.

The Foreigners

The start of the first year of full implementation of the DLP was going well, and Mrs. Duran was so excited that the school year was going more smoothly than she expected. The new DLP seemed to really be helping students succeed, which was evident in the way they were grasping both the English and Spanish languages. In fact, the English-speaking students started speaking with a Spanish accent, like their Spanish-speaking peers, and the Spanish-speaking students spoke with a little twang in their speech, which matched their English-speaking peers' speech. This acquiring of a new language in the dialect of peers helped the students bond as friends, motivating them further to learn the two languages.

What was also wonderful was that the DLP teachers were having a successful start of teaching such a rigorous curriculum in 90+ days instead of 180+ days. Even the other teachers on campus were all having successes with their students, which made the campus a fun and happy place to learn for the students. Regrettably, not everyone was feeling the happiness, and one new teacher was drowning because of one particular demanding parent.

Ms. Paige Pauly was elated when she was able to land a job right after graduation. Her studies were in early childhood, and she was certified in both early childhood and ESL, so becoming an ESL Pre-K teacher was her dream position. Upon earning this dream, she stayed up late several evenings making bulletin boards, games, centers, and nametags and setting up her room. She loved her students, and she would regularly stay up late preparing fun and exciting activities for her students. Also, she was so excited to be a part of a fledgling DLP.

Every student was dear and easy to work with, but from the start of the year, one particular student, Jerrick, proved to be challenging. Although Ms. Pauly welcomed the challenge of working with Jerrick, it seemed that he was a pleasure and would accept corrective criticism during school hours, but once his mother came to pick him up after school, Jerrick's demeanor would change drastically to the point of looking as if he was afraid of his mother, Ms. Jones. He would then tell his mother how his day went, which she would routinely spin into a day that was far from what Jerrick would relay.

Ms. Jones routinely yelled at Ms. Pauly, telling her she was too young to teach and her son deserved better. She accused Ms. Pauly of many things, such as being a sexist, a racist, and an incompetent. It seemed she took pleasure in berating Ms. Pauly in front of the parents and the other children daily, to the point that other parents began complaining to Dr. Mins about Ms. Jones's constant verbal assaults. However, Ms. Pauly was afraid to go to Dr. Mins because she was scared that not being able to handle a parent would reflect badly on her evaluation.

Dr. Mins understood that a new teacher should never be left to defend herself from a bully parent, so she quickly became involved after she was told about the verbal assaults, always supporting Ms. Pauly, and even banning Ms. Jones from the campus for a week at a time. After each ban, Ms. Jones's behavior was subdued, until an innocuous event set her off, like the lunch ladies giving Jerrick a free lunch when his lunch account totaled $0.00 or when Ms. Pauly bought popcorn for each student in the Pre-K

DLP from the fifth grade student council one Friday afternoon. Ms. Pauly and the cafeteria staff were accused of being racists as Ms. Jones believed the only reason they bought her son lunch and popcorn was because they thought he was a *"poor black kid."*

As there were only two Pre-K teachers on campus, Mrs. Duran suggested that Jerrick be placed in her room, solely, for the remainder of the year. Jerrick would be able to get both English and Spanish in Mrs. Duran's classroom, so that he would not get behind, and Ms. Pauly would hopefully have a chance to enjoy her first year of teaching. This change was thoroughly explained to Ms. Jones, and both teachers felt that as Jerrick had done so well in the DLP so far, he would continue to progress. Ms. Jones agreed to the new placement and made it clear that *"Maybe now my son will actually learn something from a good teacher!"*

It did not take long before the complaints began, unfortunately. In fact one particular incident became so out of hand and ended up in a lawsuit. The incident took place the week before Christmas break. One day after school, the parents were waiting outside the Pre-K wing, as they always did, as each Pre-K teacher led the students to their parents. When Ms. Jones saw Mrs. Duran, she approached her and angrily shouted that she wanted to speak to her about the way she taught. Mrs. Duran asked Ms. Jones to please wait after all of her students were picked up from their parents, so she could give her her undivided and private attention. Mrs. Jones demanded that the undivided and private attention take place right then and there.

At this moment, Dr. Mins walked up and asked a nearby reading recovery teacher to help make sure that Mrs. Duran's students were taken safely to their parents. Mrs. Mins then turned to Ms. Jones and Mrs. Duran and asked them to follow her into Mrs. Duran's classroom as it was close by. Ms. Jones refused shouting, *"NO! You are not going to try to lie to me like you always do!"* Again, Dr. Mins tried to calm Ms. Jones, asking her to bring her concerns to a more private venue. At that, Ms. Jones shouted, *"Maybe you need to stop lying, telling me my son would do better in her class. But, he has done worse because she is too old and he is stuck with a bunch of foreigners!"* Dr. Mins told Ms. Jones that her words were cutting and unnecessary and if she felt the need to continue with her baseless rant in front of the other students, parents, and teachers, the police would be called. Abruptly, Ms. Jones ended the conversation by stating she would leave and never return to this school, but she would go to the superintendent to report the sexist, racist, and unspeakable treatment that she and Jerrick had had to endure.

Ms. Jones stomped off school grounds as parents continued to gather their children and take them home. A large crowd of teachers, students, and parents witnessed the exchange. Dr. Mins walked a shaken Mrs. Duran to her classroom and reassured her that she had done nothing wrong and that all would be straightened out. Dr. Mins then walked to her office and called her assistant superintendent to report the incident that just occurred and to give a heads-up that Ms. Jones would be contacting the superintendent's office.

After months of an exhausting grievance process at Arthur Schools, Ms. Jones filed a lawsuit claiming that the educators unfairly treated Jerrick due to his black skin color. Other allegations included that the Spanish-speaking students received more opportunities for a better education than did Jerrick and that he did not learn anything while in the Prek-K DLP, which puts him behind as a kindergartener. Mrs. Mins wondered what could have been done to prevent this situation and how the children who were excelling in the DLP would be affected. She wanted the DLP to be a success for all students, so she and the other DLP teachers would need to discuss possible changes, if any.

WHAT ELSE DO I NEED TO KNOW?

The following is a brief insight into the issues presented in the case study, with a brief literature review to help give context to those issues.

Early Childhood and Language Learners

Young learners have many opportunities to learn at the elementary level. There are special programs that focus on language, social, emotional, and academic development from as early as three years old, such as early childhood education (ECE), ESL, and bilingual education. These special programs help students to become successful and, in some cases, they help a student to become successful in more than one language. Each is briefly explained as follows.

Early Childhood Education

ECE is called by different names depending on the state that the program resides in, but regardless of the name, ECE is for young learners from ages three to eight. For example, Colker (2009) defined pre-kindergarten as a set of programs that prepare young students for kindergarten, who will be successful by third grade, and "All pre-K programs have three characteristics in common. They are (1) governed by high program standards, (2) serve 4- year-olds or sometimes both 3- and 4- year–olds, and (3) focus on school readiness." (p. 22)

Other definitions are similar to Colker's. The UNESCO (2014) definition for "early childhood is defined as the period from birth to eight years old. A time of remarkable brain growth, these years lay the foundation for subsequent learning and development" (para 1). While the

U.S. Department of Education's Eric Thesaurus (1966a) defines ECE as "Activities and/or experiences that are intended to effect developmental changes in children, from birth through the primary units of elementary school (grades k–3"; para 1).

Therefore, qualified children at age three through eight years may begin school through an ECE program with the main focus being to prepare young students to be ready for school and successful in their academics. Although ECE programs are not considered a prerequisite course before a student enrolls in kindergarten or first grade, it is a program that is available to help those participating students become better prepared for kindergarten through third grade.

Most ECE programs have requirements to be met for a child to qualify to receive services. Those requirements may include a student's having a handicap or disability, having limited English proficiency, being a military dependent, being homeless, being classified as "poor" or having a low socioeconomic status, and/or being a ward of the state. Depending on the school district, ECE programs may be half-day or full-day, and they may allow for educators who work for the district to place their child in an ECE program, even if the child does not meet the requirements, as long as the educator parent pays for the service.

English as a Second Language

ESL is a program that helps English-language learners (ELLs) to become proficient in the English language. ESL has been defined at the federal and state levels, and the definitions focus on the ELL. For example, the U.S. Department of Education's Eric Thesaurus (1966b) defines ELLs as " Students whose first language is not English and who are in the process of learning English. Emphasis is on development of English skills, not on the limited proficiency" (para 1).

Some examples of how states define ESL or ELL aligns with the Department or Agency of Education definition. In Texas, ESL focuses on the ELL and is defined as "A person who is in the process of acquiring English and has another language as the first native language. The terms *English-language learner* and *limited-English-proficient student* are used interchangeably" (Texas Administrative Code §89.1203). The Vermont Agency of Education spells out how each school district should identify ELLs for services in ESL:

> State and local education agencies are required by law to identify English language learners (ELLs) who require language and academic support services. Students from linguistically diverse backgrounds should be assessed to determine their level of (academic) English language proficiency. (para 11)

And, the New York City Department of Education provides student support to ELLs: "We are dedicated to serving the needs of English Language Learners (ELLs)—students who speak a language other than English at home and score below proficient on English assessments when they enter our school system" (para 1).

For students who are learning English as a second language, a possible placement would be in an ESL and/or ELL classroom; this special program can be found on both elementary and secondary campuses. Students who speak a language other than English and who do not write and read English proficiently would qualify for the ESL and/or ELL program. In many states, schools have parents complete a Home Language Survey, which asks a series of questions that identify the primary language spoken in the home. If the primary language is not English, the ESL/ELL teacher and/or coordinator will make contact with the child and the child's family to determine whether the student needs specialized courses to learn English.

An English-speaking teacher is charged with helping students to learn the basic English and language arts skills needed for a student to acquire the English language and transfer this skill to academic success. An ESL/ELL program can be a self-contained classroom or a sheltered classroom, or it can be a pull-out program, where students leave their core class, usually ELA (English/Language Arts, and go to the ESL/ELL classroom. It can also be a program where co-teaching lessons are presented in a general education classroom by both the general education teacher and the ESL/ELL teacher. The main purpose is to inculcate the student in everything that deals with the English language.

The Dual-Language Program

Bilingual education is a special program that focuses on helping students who do not speak, read, or write English to become proficient in it while also becoming proficient in a second language (which in many cases is the primary language spoken at home). In several school districts, a bilingual program will be offered only if fifteen to twenty students who speak the same foreign language are identified. If fewer than the required number are identified, those students would be placed in an ESL/ELL program to receive English-language services. A bilingual classroom can appear different depending on the needs of the students in a particular school district and on a particular school campus. One program that is a becoming more prolific on school campuses is the DLP. As Lindholm-Leary (2012) noted,

> Dual-language education (DLE) programs, also known as two-way immersion, integrate English language learners (ELLs) from a common native language background (e.g., Spanish, Mandarin) and native English-speaking (NES)

students in the same classroom for academic instruction through both languages. (p. 257)

Alanis and Rodriguez (2008) have a more concise definition: "In dual-language education, two languages are used in the classroom for instruction and learning" (p. 306).

Although there are many types of DLPs and many ways a teacher can deliver instruction in a DLP, the most common, yet most expensive, is the two-way DLP, in which two languages are taught throughout a school year.

In a dual-language classroom, high levels of student engagement and student learning can be seen, and being bilingual "enhances memory and makes it easier to pay attention" (Maxwell, 2015, p. 22). DLPs can be designed to meet the needs of the student population found within a school district. Some DLPs are divided into percentages where a percentage of the time is spent on students learning English, and the rest of the percentage of time is spent on students learning another language. For example, a DLP could follow the 50/50 model, meaning that 50% of the time the students are learning English and 50% of the time the students are learning Spanish. In another classroom, a 60/40 model may be used, where 60% of the time students are learning English and 40% of the time students are learning Spanish. Regardless of what type of DLP model is implemented, it is good to remember that "the dual-language bilingual program represents a pluralistic view of language" (as cited in Alanis & Rodriguez, 2008, p. 306).

Ideally, if a school adopts the 50/50 DLP model, an ESL teacher would teach the English portion, and a bilingual teacher would teach the second language (e.g., Spanish, German, Vietnamese). Additionally, two different classrooms would house the ESL and bilingual teacher so that students would be immersed in only one language per academic classroom.

> The power of a dual-language program is not just in its additive nature but in the pedagogical equity that exists for both language groups. It is not enough to merely adjust the language of instruction; teachers must adjust their philosophy, their teaching strategies, and their view of ELs. (Alanis, & Rodriguez, 2008, p. 316)

Finally, these two teachers would share the same students and would assess their progress in both languages throughout the school year.

To qualify for a DLP placement, identified bilingual students would be automatically placed in a DLP classroom, while the English speakers would go through a screening process that would foretell whether the student and family are prepared to commit to the program for up to six years. Many bilingual and DLPs begin at the Pre-K or kindergarten level and have the student proceed in DLP classrooms through fifth or sixth grade. The long-term commitment allows students to learn a language proficiently. Additionally, the student becomes proficient in reading, writing, and speaking two languages within this time and may be better prepared to learn a third language as he/she enters high school. Finally, a contract is usually signed by the student, parent, and educators at a school that simply states that all concerned will work toward helping the student become proficient in two languages through tutoring, help with homework, parent nights, teacher-parent conferences, and other meetings.

There must be a clear dedication by the administration, the students, parents, and of course, the teachers for a DLP to work successfully. It takes a great deal of time to establish and a lot of effort to sustain. Parents need to understand the demands of the DLP so that they are prepared to help their children. Some barriers to and challenges of providing a DLP can be alleviated with the dedication from the faculty, parents, and students. However, the demanding and rigorous pace of the curriculum and other concerns include "issues related to program design, accountability, curriculum and instruction as related to biliteracy, and bilingual language development" (Lindholm-Leary, 2012, p. 258).

Working with Parents

Some say that public education is great except for the parents. Working with parents can be the easiest part of an educator's job, because the educator and parent have a very important and common interest: the student. The educator makes the relationship easy by constantly communicating to the parents about the student's progress, behavior, and other insight and by showing genuine support and dedication in providing the best educational opportunities. The parent can help to make the relationship collaborative by also communicating with the educators and student how important an education is and that respecting and supporting the teacher will help the student to have the best educational experience. It is when this mutual partnership is taken for granted or is impugned that things begin to deteriorate. There will be times when educators and parents do not agree and, when that happens, it is good to employ the techniques of *Crucial Conversations*.

Simply, *crucial conversations* are a set of skills that can be employed by people who are dedicated in mastering high-stakes crucial conversations. It is based on research that focuses on the improvement of organizational performance through the development of the major component skills:

- Get Unstuck;
- Start With Heart;
- Master My Stories;

- State My Path;
- Learn to Look;
- Make It Safe I and II;
- Explore Others' Paths; and
- Move to Action.

(Patterson et al., 2011)

"At the heart of almost all chronic problems in our organizations, our teams, and our relationships lie crucial conversations—ones that we're either not holding or not holding well" (Patterson et al., 2011, p. 9). For some educators and parents, Crucial Conversations are necessary when the stakes are high, emotions are strong, and opposing opinions are evident. Once the conversation is employed, both parties can work toward achieving a common goal that will be in the best interest of each person affected.

For more information on Crucial Conversations, please visit https://www.vitalsmarts.com/products-solutions/crucial-conversations/

NCZ—NO CONSEQUENCE ZONE

Answer the questions below by applying what you know about this case and thinking about the steps you would take if you were faced with this situation or a similar one.

1 First-year teachers are overwhelmed in the first few months.
   a. What policies and procedures are in place in your school district that help first-year teachers succeed in their first year?
   b. If there are no policies and procedures, what would be the best plan of action to help first-year teachers succeed?
   c. What is the best and most professional plan to prepare first-year teachers when dealing with difficult parents?
2 Parents will threaten to go to your boss, to go to the media, and to take you to court.
   a. If a parent threatens you, what steps would you take to calm the parent, and when would you report the parent to your superiors?
   b. When would you report the parent to the school resource officer or city police officer?
3 Parents can be difficult and may try everyone's patience on a campus.
   a. How can educators turn a difficult parent situation into a positive one?
   b. Think about what the parents are upset about and find the root of their displeasure. What can you do to help them work through that displeasure, so that they are at least cordial with all staff on a campus?

4 Implementing a new program on a campus is exciting, overwhelming, and time-consuming. For this reason, a plan of action or steps toward implementation should be discussed and written with all stakeholders.

   a. What steps must be taken before asking other educators, parents, students, and the district administrators to buy in to the implementation process?

   b. Discuss how money can be spent: specifically, from what funds can money be spent on a new program?

   c. How should the Arthur School District handle allowing students who move into the district and want to join the DLP in grades other than Pre-K?

   d. What type of budgetary considerations need to be made when implementing a new program?

REFERENCES

Alanis, I., & Rodriguez, M. A. (2008). Sustaining a dual-language immersion program: Features of success. *Journal of Latinos & Education*, 7(4), 305–319.

Colker, L. J. (2009). Pre-K (What exactly is it?). *Teaching Young Children*, 2(1), 22–24.

Lindholm-Leary, K. (2012). Success and challenges in dual-language education. *Theory Into Practice*, 51(4), 256–262.

Maxwell, L. A. (2015). Successes spur push for dual-language classes. *Education Digest*, 80(6),19–24.

New York City Department of Education. (2015). English language learners. Retrieved from http://schools.nyc.gov/Academics/ELL/default.htm

Patterson, K., Grenny, J., McMillan, R., & Switzler, A. (2011). *Crucial conversations* (2nd ed.). New York: McGraw-Hill, Inc.

Texas Administrative Code, Chapter 89, Subchapter BB, §89.1203

UNESCO. (2014). Early childhood care and education. Retrieved from http://www.unesco.org/new/en/education/themes/strengthening-education-systems/early-childhood

U.S. Department of Education. (1966a). ERIC thesaurus: Early childhood education. Retrieved from http://eric.ed.gov/?ti=Early+Childhood+Education

U.S. Department of Education. (1966b). ERIC thesaurus: English language learners. Retrieved from http://eric.ed.gov/?ti=English+Language+Learners

Vermont Agency of Education. (2015). English Language Learners (ELL). Retrieved from http://education.vermont.gov/english-language-learner

Chapter 9

Mom Is Too Cool

Parental involvement on a campus can be a great idea when the parents are vetted and are trusted to do what is expected. Parents on campuses are a welcome sight, and their presence is encouraged, especially if student success can be linked to parental visibility. A problem arises when a parent may have been vetted and trusted but violates that trust by unspeakable actions. This one parent may cause such a ripple effect that educators may become overly cautious by decreasing the opportunities for welcoming parents on campus.

Contingency plans should be in place at each campus to help educators follow an approved plan of action to remove from campus parents who violate the school's rules. These plans should also include the help of the school resource officer (SRO), especially if criminal activity is suspected. Unfortunately, trusting all parents to do the right thing by both their own child and the other students on a campus is not always what occurs. As this case presents, one parent can make educators skeptical of all parents.

THE CASE

The Mom: Ms. Julie Hayworth

Ms. Julie Hayworth grew up in Roswell, USA and graduated from Roswell High School (RHS), where her daughter now attends. Ms. Hayworth was the captain of the dance team and salutatorian of her class and earned a full scholarship to a renowned out-of-state university. Her life was perfect, and she could not wait to leave Roswell for "better" things.

During Julie's senior year seventeen years ago, she became pregnant by her longtime boyfriend, Blain. She was so excited about being pregnant, especially as Blain asked her to marry him—because he thought it was the right thing to do—and take her to Austin, Texas with him; he was going to make it big in the music industry, and Austin seemed to be a great place to try out his dream. Julie immediately vacated her plans to attend the out-of-state university and made plans to move to Texas.

However, when graduation came, Blain's parents told Mr. and Mrs. Hayworth, Julie's parents, that they would help pay for any costs that Julie would have arising from the keeping of her baby, but that Blain would be going to Texas alone. They were not going to allow Julie to ruin their son's life by purposefully becoming pregnant; yet, they wanted to be a part of the baby's life. Blain wanted to go to Austin and knew he was not ready to settle down with a wife and baby. Even though he loved Julie, he was glad that his parents stepped in on his behalf and that he did not have to go through with a marriage.

Devastated, Julie had nowhere to go but to stay at home with her parents and her new baby, which she delivered three weeks after graduation. Because of Blain's initial promise to take her to Texas, Julie had declined her out-of-state university's acceptance to pursue becoming a mother and wife. Julie found herself stuck at home with her parents, who helped raise her daughter as she went to the local community college and then to a local state school.

The Assistant Principal

Dr. Melissa Shoemaker is in her fifth year as an assistant principal at Roswell High School. She has had a very successful career as both a teacher and an assistant principal (AP), mainly because she is perceived to be fair, consistent, and a believer of school board–established policies and rules. Her goal as an educator was to help students and teachers understand that when policies and rules are followed, positive consequences are inevitable. Additionally, she wants students who are about to leave public education and enter adulthood to appreciate, adhere to, and understand how following rules, policies, and laws are a part of taking responsibility and promoting self-worth and growth within a society.

Dr. Shoemaker is respected and is even feared by many students, because although she does take into account an individual student's circumstance, if a rule is broken, negative consequences will follow. For example, a freshman male brought a ten-inch butcher knife to school to use against a bully. His best friend was afraid for him and reported him to Dr. Shoemaker. Immediately, Dr. Shoemaker called for the School Resource Officer (SRO) and requested that he accompany her to the classroom. Both Dr. Shoemaker and the SRO entered the classroom, asked the student to follow them to Dr. Shoemaker's office, and Dr. Shoemaker proceeded to search for the knife, which she found in the book bag. When asked why he brought the knife, the freshman male confessed that he was being bullied and wanted to take care of the bully once and for all. However, he never notified a teacher, administrator, his parents, or any other adult about the bully. According to both the Student Code of Conduct (SCOC) and the state penal code, the freshman male committed a felony by bringing an illegal knife into a weapon-free school zone. These violations of the SCOC and the penal code landed the student in a disciplinary alternative school.

Yes, Dr. Shoemaker is a good administrator, and she has been a positive addition to RHS. Five years ago, when Dr. Shoemaker came to Roswell, USA, she was not sure she was going to like the small town, as she spent most of her life in large cities and school districts. However, she found that kids are very similar from school to school, and she has grown to love her home in Roswell. She has really enjoyed the collaborative partnerships she has with the teachers and parents, which have made her job an easier and fun one.

However, Dr. Shoemaker found that there are some "helicopter" parents, those who swoop down to "save" their children from responsibility, and a new type of parent: The buddy parent. Dr. Shoemaker had not come across the buddy parent in her years in education but recently found that a handful of parents wanted to be their child's "buddy" more than their parent. This small group of parents were seen as dressing in clothes that high school students would typically wear, wearing makeup/cologne that was too strong, and getting piercings and tattoos in the most noticeable areas on their bodies. They also spoke the same colloquial language as their kids, emulating their high school children as much as possible. This new fad of parenting was alarming to see on campus, but as their numbers were few, Dr. Shoemaker did not expect to have too much trouble with them.

The Buddy Mom and the Party

One particular parent, Ms. Julie Hayworth, has exceeded this definition to the point of behaving more like a teenage best friend to her daughter than like a mom. Ms. Hayworth behaves as if she is a student attending RHS, which is evident in the way she dresses and flirts with the boys. She has a daughter, Cassidy, who is in the ninth grade, a good-natured, respectful, hard-working student. Cassidy is on the junior varsity cheerleading squad, and she is a freshmen representative on the student council. She has enjoyed her freshman year so far and is grateful that she has a supportive mom.

Roswell High is a closed campus, which means that all students are required to eat lunch on campus, and they are not allowed to leave the campus without permission. For this reason, Ms. Hayworth started coming up to eat lunch, sporadically, with Cassidy about a month ago, but lately she has started to come every day. At first, she would bring lunch to Cassidy and sit with her at a lunch table, just the two of them, throughout the lunch period. As the weeks passed, however, Ms. Hayworth began to eat lunch with Cassidy and her friends. She also started to bring enough food for all of Cassidy's lunch table friends, which included a group of boys who are sophomores and juniors.

The principal divided the student population equally among the four APs, which meant that an AP would take care of all matters concerning the assigned students. As Cassidy was assigned to Dr. Shoemaker, she was charged to speak to Ms. Hayworth whenever an issue arose. While Dr. Shoemaker was on lunch duty, she noticed that Ms. Hayworth was feeding many students with commercial food, so she explained that according to district policy, only outside, bought food for Cassidy was acceptable, and any food for any other child could be accepted only if the parents of the other students wrote a letter stating it was okay for Ms. Hayworth to bring them food at lunchtime. Hence, Ms. Hayworth told Cassidy's friends, if they wanted food brought, they would need to get their parent's to sign a letter stating it was okay to eat food not sold by the school. When Ms. Hayworth had all of the letters gathered, she gave them to Dr. Shoemaker, and there was no longer a problem with her bringing food for all of Cassidy's friends.

However, other curious things were also occurring. First, Ms. Hayworth was not dressing as the professional that many thought she was. She worked with her mother and father at their family accounting firm; hence, she used to come to school in business dress. Lately, though, she had been coming to lunch in provocative clothing, which included tight jeans, see through tops, low-cut tops, very short skirts, and six-inch heels. She also started wearing much more makeup than usual, and she fixed her hair in a style that was commonly worn by the female students.

Second, Ms. Hayworth was no longer eating lunch with Cassidy. She would bring food for Cassidy's friends and even sit at the same table as Cassidy, but she would sit in the middle of the boys, who were very flirtatious with her. This bothered the teachers and administrators on duty, and when Dr. Shoemaker was notified of the inappropriate behavior that was being observed, she asked Ms. Hayworth to come see her in her office.

During the meeting, Dr. Shoemaker thanked Ms. Hayworth for being such a great support of the students and thanked her for her tireless efforts and money in keeping the students fed. She also remarked on Cassidy's success at school, stating that she was impressed with the great progress Cassidy was making with her coursework and with her elective activities. Dr. Shoemaker then let Ms. Hayworth know that she would like to encourage her to come to lunch; however, if she continued, she would need to sit with Cassidy to show that she is there for her daughter and not other non-familial students. It was also explained that the observations from other teachers and administrators was a bit uneasy and they felt the closeness to the boys was inappropriate. Finally, Ms. Hayworth's dress was spoken of, and Dr. Shoemaker asked Ms. Hayworth to follow the same dress code that is required by the teachers, which aligns more with Ms. Hayworth's business dress attire.

Ms. Hayworth then spoke and stated that she did not realize that she had been such a topic of conversation and that this confrontation embarrassed her. She stated that she is first and foremost at school for Cassidy but that the other kids love and treat her like their own moms, which she admitted to loving, so she obliged their attempts to get closer to her by allowing them to call her their "Buddy Mom." She further explained that the kids wanted her to be a part of the "cool crowd," and that meant to sit in the middle of all of the students, not just the boys. Again, she told of how embarrassed she was and stated that she would not come as often to lunch and would promise to dress in professional dress whenever she came to campus. Both Dr. Shoemaker and Ms. Hayworth concluded the meeting amicably and with the understanding that the lunchtime would no longer be a point of contention or inappropriateness.

The Incident

Weeks had passed since Dr. Shoemaker had seen Ms. Hayworth on campus, and when she checked in on Cassidy, everything seemed back to normal. Cassidy was such a great kid that Dr. Shoemaker felt that she was so well adjusted and happy that she would be able to weather anything that came her way. She even made a point to say hello to Cassidy and ask how her mother was whenever she saw her in the hallways, to which Cassidy always responded, "I'm doing well. My mom is well, too."

When Ms. Hayworth finally did come on campus during lunch, as promised, she dressed professionally and sat next to Cassidy. She also continued to bring Cassidy's friends lunch, but she also started bringing water bottles and snacks to the other kids, which seemed harmless. Dr. Shoemaker and the other educators on duty felt better about the situation, especially as Ms. Hayworth never stayed more than ten minutes and always sat right next to Cassidy.

Dr. Shoemaker had also thought that everything with Cassidy's friends, specifically the boys from her lunch table, was going well. They had not shown any signs of missing Ms. Hayworth, nor did they comment or ask why she did not come to lunch anymore whenever Dr. Shoemaker walked over to their lunch table during lunchtime. Therefore, all seemed very well.

A day in spring changed all of Dr. Shoemaker's insight, however. She had received a call from an angry, concerned parent whose daughter attended a party at Ms. Hayworth's house over the past weekend. The parent stated, "My daughter went over to that whore's house and was served beer. What will you do about this!"

Dr. Shoemaker asked the parent to clarify who the "whore" was and who served the beer. The parent continued,

> My daughter says that Ms. Hayworth invited a whole bunch of boys over to her house over the weekend when Cassidy would be visiting her dad. When the boys came over, they brought some girls with them, which included my daughter. They were then told that there was beer and margaritas in the refrigerator and that everyone was welcome to get drunk and stay the night if they couldn't drive home. My daughter sure as hell got drunk and didn't come home until five yesterday morning.

When Dr. Shoemaker asked whether she called the police, the parent stated, "I'm not an idiot! Of course I did, but I also wanted you to know so you could do something too."

The parent then continued,

> Did you know that Ms. Hayworth is also bringing alcohol on campus? According to my daughter, she brings it to a group of boys who she eats lunch with, and disguises the alcohol in the water bottles she brings. From what my daughter and her friends are saying, she puts vodka in the water, because it doesn't smell like beer does and it is colorless. She even supplies them with water bottles that are just full of vodka, and no water. AND, the snacks she provides to the kids; have you noticed deformed gummi bears? Those have been soaked in vodka!

Dr. Shoemaker was stunned and could not believe that she had not realized that Ms. Hayworth was possibly bringing alcohol on campus to give to minors. She felt so stupid, especially as she had been purposefully going to the lunch table to check on Cassidy and her friends. She was disappointed in herself but also in Ms. Hayworth.

First, Dr. Shoemaker met with her principal, the other APs, and the two SROs to brief them of what she learned from the angry, concerned parent. She then divulged her plan of action, which included speaking to each student from the lunch table and searching their bags and lockers for the infamous water bottles and gummi bears. The contents would need to be checked to confirm the parent's allegations. The other APs and SROs agreed to help.

After the APs and the SROs conducted their investigations, they found the following information, with some verbatim quotes from the students below:

1 Cassidy broke down and cried when she was told of the allegation. She had no knowledge of what her mother was doing and felt betrayed that she had a party with her friends while she was with her dad.

2 The boys and some girls from the lunch table, seven total, all confessed that Ms. Hayworth had been bringing them alcohol for almost as long as she had been coming to lunch. They made a promise to Ms. Hayworth that if she bought them alcohol, they would never let Cassidy know. In return, Ms. Hayworth would allow them to go to her house to party when Cassidy was visiting her dad.

3 The party last weekend was just one of many parties that Ms. Hayworth had when Cassidy was gone for the weekend. They remember at least five in the fall-winter semester alone, and each party got a little bit raunchier than the next. For example, couples were "hooking up" and having sex in different rooms. Also, when one of the kids asked to bring marijuana to the parties, Ms. Hayworth allowed it, but it could be smoked only on the back patio.

4 Ms. Hayworth was becoming more involved with each new party. At first, she played the host, but then she started dressing like a "hooker" and started "…grinding on all of us boys. So, we started grinding back." Three boys admitted to having a sexual encounter with Ms. Hayworth, which they stressed was only fellatio, "…so it wasn't really sex."

5 All seven students were supposed to keep the parties a secret. They created a little secret society, but one of the seven had a nosey sister who got drunk last weekend and told her mother all about the party she attended.

6 Some of the seven had pictures of the students drinking with Ms. Hayworth at her house. One student even videoed Ms. Hayworth performing fellatio on another, but that student is eighteen, so "the sex was consensual; no harm done."

7 During all these confessions, the nosey sister texted her friends that she was in big trouble, and she quickly texted about her weekend experience at Ms. Hayworth's house, which became the fastest-traveled text throughout RHS and the school district.

Dr. Shoemaker was devastated. Where was she to go from here? How did this happen while she thought all was under control? What were the signs that she clearly missed? Together, the APs and SROs took their findings to the principal, and the next steps were laid out.

WHAT ELSE DO I NEED TO KNOW?

The following is a brief insight into the issues presented in the case study, with a brief literature review to help give context to those issues.

The Buddy Parent

The buddy parent is one that is permissive but dangerously so. This parent behaves like an undisciplined teenager without consideration to those who may be harmed by the parent's actions. Like Ms. Hayworth, buddy parents are self-destructive, self-absorbed, and conniving. The buddy parent cannot be trusted to volunteer or to come onto the campus without wreaking havoc.

The buddy parent has evolved from the helicopter parent. Educators want parents involved but not so involved that they become helicopter parents or overly involved parents who create a dysfunctional interdependence with their child to the point the child grows up to be that adult child who believes he/she cannot succeed without parental involvement (Manos, 2009). The goal for students on any campus is to become independent and successful with guidance of parents but not full intervention. Parents who are too involved in their children's lives or who over-parent by micromanaging their children's lives have earned the monikers "helicopters, hovercrafts, hummingbirds, stealth fighters, and black hawks" (LeMoyne & Buchanan, 2011, p. 400). The buddy parent is involved too, but superficially, focusing on his/her needs and desires and on how to meet those needs and desires.

With the widespread use of electronic devices by students, parents have kept their children within reach through "the electronic umbilical cord" (LeMoyne & Buchanan, 2011, p. 400). This electronic umbilical cord has also allowed parents to keep in contact with other students on a campus. Like Ms. Hayworth, some parents have engaged in inappropriate—and sometimes illegal—relationships with students. The challenge for educators, then, is how to guide parents in helping educators "… in our mutual goal of helping students become engaged learners, competent and creative problem solvers, and responsible and effective citizens—in essence, helping students grow up" (Coburn, 2006, p. 11).

It may be easier to understand parents if we look at types of parenting styles. In LeMoyne and Buchanan's (2011) work, Baumrind's research was presented, where seven types of parenting styles were identified: permissive, authoritarian, authoritative, non-authoritarian directive, democratic, good-enough, and rejecting/neglecting (pp. 401–402).

These parenting styles shed some light on what types of parents may be present on a campus.

So, how do educators work with all types of parents, specifically the buddy parent? Although there is no research on the buddy parent, there is literature on the helicopter parent, which focuses on those who have students at the college level. Although most educators would expect that college students are old enough to navigate through the collegial waters on their own, Cutright (2008) recognized the need for intentional steps toward working collaboratively with parents. Four of his steps can be adapted at the P-12 level and are presented in part as

1   The Partnership Relationship: "develop a relationship that is a partnership with the parents and the family." This will help the parents feel like they can trust the educators on a campus.

2   Orientation as an Event and as a Process: At the P-12 level, this is called the Open House; however, taking more time to show the parents what it means for a student to be on a campus may help parents to be less dysfunctionally involved in their child's life. For example, an orientation tour could be done for all new and incoming students and their parents.

3   Handbooks and Similar Print Materials: Both students and parents should have a handbook that lists information, such as a testing calendar for the school year, a grievance policy, and other pertinent information about the school district and school. During the year, as new information is gathered, this should be mailed to the parents from a central point (i.e., from the principal's office).

4   Whom to Contact: "Most college presidents or provosts don't want to be called when the hot water in a residence hall is lacking," just as a principal shouldn't be the first person a parent contacts when a student hasn't made the coveted 'A'. Give parents the contact numbers of those whom they need to contact, or chain of command, when faced with certain occurrences. (pp. 43–46)

It is pertinent to note that the percentage of buddy and helicopter parents is small, but applying the steps above may help to lower the percentage for your campus even more. Taub's (2008) work also centered on college students, and her advice may also help public educators in working with parents. It would be good to remember that most parents

are invested in being good parents; have shared goals with educators concerning their child's success, growth, and maturity; accept educators teaching about child development, which can be helpful; and, want to be acknowledged that they have a role at school (pp. 24–25).

The key is finding that special tool that works best for your parents on your campus.

Student Off-Campus Behavior

Every SCOC should have a section that explicitly describes and defines what off-campus behavior looks like and what consequences, if any, may be applied if a violation occurs. In many states, educators do not have jurisdiction over what can be done in a private home where students and parents are concerned. Unless the situation is brought to the campus through, for instance, a text message, pictures, or gossip that disrupts the school environment, the schools will have to defer to the law enforcement agencies to investigate and make arrests as needed.

Unfortunately, some parents and students are creating unsafe environments in private homes, which brings concern to educators when these students come back to school and discuss their weekend dalliances. So, when are educators allowed to discipline students for off-campus behavior and address the parents' actions? First, for any off-campus violations of both the SCOC and penal code, a concurrent investigation should be done: one that takes place through the school and one that law enforcement will conduct. If there is a video or pictures of the incident, an arrest may be imminent if it is evident that a violation of the penal code has been made. Second, for students, a clear indication that a penal code violation has occurred would mean that a SCOC violation has also been made. Remember that your SCOC should have the most severe and expellable offenses aligned with the state penal code, which means that if they violate one code, they automatically violate the other. Finally, if criminal charges have been made against a parent, banishment from any school property accompanied by a trespass warning may be given.

Criminally, you may give trespass warnings and ban a parent from the campus or other school property. However, when banning a person from campus, it must be an all-out ban for a criminal trespass violation to be referred to and enforced by the police. In other words, you cannot allow the parent to come on campus for a parent/teacher conference and not for anything else if you want the trespass warning to have effect. If you do allow a parent on campus during their time of banishment from the campus, the trespass ban would be ineffective, and the legal system would be removed from the equation. To be sure that you are following what your state and local codes require, please check and read them thoroughly and make sure everyone involved knows about the banishment.

When it comes to disguising alcohol on campuses, students are learning new ways to get drunk at school without being caught. Some students buy licorice and soak it in vodka or other alcohol, then eat it as a snack at school. Others make homemade Jell-o, pour alcohol in the mix, chill it, then take it to school for a snack. Still others use other orifices to get drunk by inserting vodka- (or other type of alcohol-) soaked tampons vaginally or rectally. Then, there are those that just bring water or coke bottles full of alcohol and drink them throughout the day.

When it comes to sex, there are a growing number of parents who believe that allowing their child to have sex in their home is perfectly okay. Clean sheets, a safe environment, a clean bathroom to shower in afterward, and a supply of condoms are what these parents believe is best for their child to have when engaging in their first/subsequent sexual encounters. There have been some parents who have created a sex commune by allowing not only their child but also other minors to have sex in their homes. When educators are faced with these two realizations about alcohol and sexual encounters in family homes with adult permission or participation, their jobs become more complicated.

If all of this is known, when is it reasonable to discipline students for off-campus behavior? Students must be taught that they may be disciplined for actions done both on campus and off campus if a violation of either the SCOC or the penal/criminal code occurs. Additionally, in the instances where neither has been directly violated, students in extra-curricular activities, such as athletics or other competitive clubs may be disciplined through their extra-curricular teacher. Most clubs and organizations have students sign a contract that outlines a merit and demerit system. Within this system, specific violations of the contract and organization are spelled out, which gives the teacher/coach/sponsor room to discipline according to the contract. For example, if a soccer player gets drunk at a party and his or her coach finds out, he or she may be benched for a game for violating the athletic contract.

The school administrators and the SRO, as needed, will handle off-campus behavior that occurs when a student is at a school-sponsored event, such as an out-of-town sporting contest. The SCOC and the penal code are enforceable away from campus when the school pays for and sponsors students to perform at another venue; no matter whether the venue is in another state or country, the school rules would apply.

Finally, the school can discipline students who behave in an activity off campus that is reported to the police department where an arrest is made or a ticket is issued. For instance, if a group of students burgle five houses over the weekend and they get caught and arrested, the school administrators may enforce discipline through suspension, expulsion, or placement in a disciplinary alternative school even if the students go to court and are found not guilty. Administrators may still discipline the students in situations such as this based on the initial reports of illegal conduct. School district policies and guidelines will be helpful in this type of instance as they may give an administrator more options.

NCZ—NO CONSEQUENCE ZONE

Answer the questions below by applying what you know about this case and thinking about the steps you would take if you were faced with this situation or a similar one.

1 It is impossible to stop every possible criminal act on a campus. Students and parents may be committing criminal acts on campus that may never be discovered.
   a. If this statement is true, what needs to be in place to protect students from possible parental predators?
   b. What should be in place to help educators identify students with alcohol or other illegal drugs while on campus?
2 Off-campus behavior is becoming more relevant to educators and students at a school because what happens off-campus is regularly brought back to school, which may then lead to interruptions in the educational process.
   a. How do educators prevent off-campus behavior to affect the learning environment?
   b. When does an off-campus incident become a school issue and not just a police issue?
   c. What types of jurisdictions do you have as an administrator to enforce school policy for off-campus behavior at your campus?
3 Lunch policies differ from school district to school district.
   a. What is your school's lunch policy and does it help to keep students safe?
   b. Weigh the pros and cons of having a closed or open campus.
   c. What are the rules for a parent or family member to eat lunch with a student on your campus?
4 Refer to Chapter 2 under When Should Someone Have Known?!
   a. Discuss the signs or actions that a parent would have to display or exhibit in order for educators to become worried or suspicious that something untoward is occurring between a parent and a student?
   b. What do your state laws impart concerning sexual contact between minors and adults? Between adult students and adults?
5 Looking at the big picture,
   a. what are the emotional and social ramifications for Cassidy as she tries to move on with her life at Roswell High School?
   b. What are the ramifications for the all the students on campus?
   c. What are the political ramifications for the educators?

REFERENCES

Coburn, K. L. (2006). Organizing a ground crew for today's helicopter parents. *About Campus*, 11(3), 9–16.

Cutright, M. (2008). From helicopter parent to valued partner: Shaping the parental relationship for student success. *New Directions for Higher Education*, 2008(144), 39–48.

LeMoyne, T., & Buchanan, T. (2011). Does hovering matter? Helicopter parenting and its effect on well-being. *Sociological Spectrum*, 31(4), 399–418.

Manos, M. (2009). Helicopter parents: Empathetic or pathetic? *Phi Kappa Phi Forum*, 89(3), 21–21.

Taub, D. (2008). Exploring the impact of parental involvement on student development. *New Directions for Student Services*, 2008(122), 15–28.

Chapter 10

The Search for Rights

A school resource officer (SRO) is a positive icon on a campus, the presence of whom can often signal a safe campus. The SRO is also one who helps educators to keep the peace and encourages students to follow the rules/laws and succeed academically. Enforcing state and federal laws is one of the main jobs of an SRO and, when a person violates those laws on a campus, an SRO will follow procedures to try to ensure that justice is served. For example, when an SRO has probable cause to suspect a student is concealing something in violation of the law, the SRO may proceed with a search to obtain necessary evidence to support a prosecution in the case.

For school administrators, upholding the federal and state laws must also be a concern. When an SRO arrests a student, the campus administrators must follow through with their procedures of placing the student in a suspension or proceeding with a school hearing to place the student in an alternative discipline placement. Parents may legally challenge these administrative actions, questioning the actions of both the SRO and the school administration. As this case will show, it is not easy being an educator or an SRO in such a litigious environment.

THE CASE

Officer Sean O'Kelley has enjoyed his years at Coolidge High School (CHS) and, after seven years, he has grown to respect educators and their daily interactions with teenagers. He came to CHS after working with the Prairie Creek City Police Department for seventeen years. He always hoped he would end up at a school as an SRO because his passion was to help students understand that police officers are good, helpful, and dependable people that should be trusted. Throughout his seven years here, he has been working with the superintendent and other administrators to ensure that the SRO program for Prairie Creek Schools (PCS) would be implemented for services to all five high school campuses, fifteen middle school campuses, and thirty-three elementary campuses.

As Officer O'Kelley was the first SRO in PCS and, because he made such a great argument for positioning SROs on campuses to increase campus safety and security, the board of trustees approved having one SRO placed at each of the five high schools, one SRO for every two middle schools, and one SRO for every three elementaries. All twenty-three SROs would be state peace officers, which meant they would be able to carry a gun and have the powers of arrest. The board of trustees were so impressed with Officer O'Kelley's passion and dedication to the SRO program that they created their own Prairie Creek School Police Department and hired O'Kelley to serve as the chief of police.

Before the PCS trustees approved the twenty-three SROs, they worked with Chief O'Kelley to create the best SRO program to fit their community as a whole and each individual school population. To be hired, SROs had to proceed successfully through an extensive background check, fingerprinting, and psychological testing, and they were given guidelines/training. All administrators are also given this training so that they know the expectations and limitations of the SROs. A brief portion of the SRO handbook follows.

The Prairie Creek Schools School Resource Officer Program

SROs are to provide security to a school campus. Their primary focus is the prevention of crime, the enforcement of laws, and the education of those on campus about the law. The SRO will be considered as part of the campus staff and should get to know all educators, students, and parents related to their campus. All SROs will promote the guidelines outlined by the Prairie Creek Schools Board of Trustees.

- All SROs will enforce the penal code within the guidelines of their discretion, first and foremost. Security and law enforcement is the primary job of an SRO, and any search and seizures, breaking up fights, or making arrests, for example, are all duties of a peace officer and are expected of the SRO when an incident dictates.
- All SROs will be assigned to a particular school. When needed, they may be called to another school as backup and/or as additional provider of security. Additionally, SROs will be assigned to different night and weekend duties at their school's extra-curricular events and at school board meetings or other district functions as needed/scheduled.

- Visibility is paramount. All SROs should continuously be seen on campus, monitoring activities and all persons on a campus while on duty. For those who are not assigned to a single campus, visibility is expected on the days they are assigned to a campus.
- Counseling and law enforcement advice may be given to the students, staff, and parents via whole-group presentations or one-to-one educational sessions. A friendly, approachable, and accessible demeanor should be portrayed at all times.
- All SROs will have their own office and workspace. Each will have at least one computer that will have access to all school cameras, and all SROs should monitor them frequently. One secretary will be assigned to every four SROs at the elementary and middle school levels. One secretary will be assigned to each high school SRO.
- All SROs and school educators should be partners and work together to keep a campus safe and secure.
- The chain of command will be: SROs will report to Chief O'Kelley and the chief will report to the superintendent and board of trustees. All SROs will be supervised and evaluated by Chief O'Kelley, or his designees, and the superintendent and the board of trustees will supervise and evaluate Chief O'Kelley.

With all the guidelines in place, SROs were put in place for this school year and have been doing a great job in curbing violations of both the Student Code of Conduct (SCOC) and the penal code.

The Robotics Snitch

Chief O'Kelley was very impressed with the way the Prairie Creek School Board worked at getting the SROs on campus. He enjoyed visiting each campus, ensuring that each SRO understood the implementation process of the SRO program. He also felt confident that his SROs had enough professional development on how to execute the expectations of an SRO, and he just knew that whatever came their way, the SROs would do well in keeping their schools safe and secure.

During the day, the SROs make a habit of walking the halls and talking with the students while getting to know who are perceived as troublemakers and rule breakers. Their purpose is to be positive role models, providing guidance to students and educators and promoting security, such as providing a student hotline where students are able to report suspicious/inappropriate activity anonymously to the SRO through a phone message, text, or e-mail. When a report comes to an SRO and after assessing whether the allegation is a penal code violation, the SRO takes the report to an assistant principal (AP). Together, they formulate a plan of action to work through the anonymous tip.

In a recent event, an eighth grade student e-mailed his SRO, Officer Mark Cheney, and reported that he knew of a drug ring occurring on campus at CHS. The student named three students and observations of what has happened in the last two weeks to him and a friend. The e-mail contained the following:

> My name is Brad Tracey. I am an 8th grader at Pike Middle School and I go to Coolidge High School for Robotics class. My friend is Zach Jacobs and he goes to Robotics class too. We mind our own business at CHS, but these three guys keep bothering us. They are Jerry Faze, Ronald Meyers, and Denzel Powers. They told us they were going to beat us up when we used the bathroom and when we were in the hall going to our bus. We don't use the bathroom anymore at Coolidge. Zach and I told them we weren't going to sell any drugs the last time we saw them, which was yesterday. But, we are really nervous that they are going to use a gun or knife on us, because they showed us that they have these weapons at school. They said we were going to die if we didn't do what they want. We don't want to die. My dad has a gun I can use, but I don't want to get in trouble. Can you help us?

Officer Cheney contacted the CHS SRO, Officer Kasey McLaughlin, and they discussed a plan of action. Officer Kasey knew the three high school students identified in the e-mail, two of whom are sophomores (Jerry [fifteen years old] and Ronald [sixteen years old]) and one of whom is a junior (Denzel [eighteen years old]). He had arrested Jerry last year for having marijuana and a switchblade on his person once and made another arrest this year for disruption of the learning environment after he was yelling at a teacher, calling her profane words during a math class.

Officer Kasey did not know Ronald very well, as Ronald had just moved to CHS from out of state just after Christmas break. However, Officer Kasey knew Denzel very well. Denzel had an arrest record that started when he was in seventh grade. His record included petty theft, vandalism, possession of narcotics, domestic violence (against his mother and younger sister), fighting on school grounds, and disruption of the learning environment. He was recognized as one of the ringleaders of a gang operating at CHS. This gang was believed to be able to get drugs on campus and was selling to other students. Unfortunately, the intelligence gathered on the gang had not yet turned into probable cause or an arrestable offense.

Officer Cheney and Officer Kasey met with their respective APs and the following was accomplished:

1 The plan of action: Chief O'Kelley was notified and told of the situation and of the plan of action, which he approved. The CHS APs (four total) and Officer Kasey went to each individual high school student's classroom, had each gather their things, and took each to the APs'

office. The APs and Officer Kasey walked behind each, escorting them to the APs' office so that they could see them at all times, especially looking for any attempts to get rid of evidence. Once in the APs' office, all were individually told that a tip was given about their alleged drug activity and weapons on campus.

2   Ronald and Jerry were separated and placed in different offices with an AP. In each room, the AP reminded the individuals of the tip that they had received and elaborated by telling that allegations of coercion to sell drugs was occurring on campus, including threats involving a weapon. They were told to write a statement about their knowledge of any drug activity on campus, which should include names, times, places, and types of drugs. After the statements were written and seeking a verbal answer, the AP asked each student questions about what was written and again verbally asked what each knew about any drug activity or weapons on campus. This was done purposefully to see whether there was any discrepancy between the verbal and written statements; there were several.

3   AP Tony Sears and Officer Kasey questioned Denzel in a third office after he wrote his statement. SRO Kasey stood in the back of the room while AP Sears conducted the verbal questioning. AP Sears asked Denzel whether there was anything that he wanted to say about the allegation of weapons and drugs on campus. Denzel stated, "*You can read can't you? Then read my statement!*" His statement read, "*I don't know nothin about no drugs on campus.*" Then, Mr. Sears told him that he would be searched and anything on his person, in his locker, or in his car that is illegal or prohibited would be seized. Denzel was directed to empty his pockets, but he refused, stating that he had rights that were being violated. When Mr. Sears asked which rights were being violated, Denzel just repeated that his rights were being violated. Mr. Sears then reminded Denzel that per the SCOC, he had every right to search and to seize anything that was found to be illegal or prohibited in a student's possession. Denzel continued to refuse to be searched and demanded that Mr. Sears call his dad and ask his permission before he searched anything else. At that, Mr. Sears told Denzel that he would go ahead and search his locker instead, as that was school property; Denzel continued to protest the search.

4   At the middle school, Officer Cheney and AP Teri Walker called Brad and Zach individually to the AP's office. They asked the boys to write a statement pertaining to the details that were in the e-mail that Brad had sent. They asked for specific times, dates, places, observations, dialogue, and actions. After Brad and Zach wrote their statements, they were asked to sign and date them. They were individually questioned verbally about what had occurred within the last two weeks and whether

any witnesses were available to write statements on their behalf. Both boys stated that no other witnesses were available as the three high school boys always caught them when no one else was around. Both of these verbal and written statements were aligned.

5 Back at the high school, Mr. Sears and Officer Kasey walked Denzel to his locker, which was in the hallway where English classrooms are located. Fifth period had just started, so the hallway was clear throughout the entire process. At the locker, Denzel refused to open it, citing again that his rights were being violated and voicing that neither he nor his parents gave anyone permission to search his locker. Mr. Sears acknowledged hearing what Denzel stated and repeated that according to the SCOC, he has the right to search any student and any student's possessions; hence, Mr. Sears cut off the lock and began the search. At first, nothing seemed amiss because the locker was full of textbooks, notebooks, and tennis shoes. However, as Mr. Sears removed each schoolbook, he opened them by exposing the spine and found three marijuana "joints" in three textbooks. As he continued to search, he noticed that the back locker wall and the locker ceiling seams appeared bent. As he investigated by running his fingers across the seam, he felt something between the two locker walls. As he pulled on what seemed to be paper, a wad of cash held by a rubber band materialized, and a list of drugs sold and money collected was attached. Because this search by Mr. Sears turned up illegal drugs, a law violation, Officer Kasey began the process of arresting Denzel for the offense of possession of drugs and had him spread his legs and arms apart, calling in the arrest to dispatch. He called for one of the SROs from another school to back him up at CHS.

6 After Denzel was told he was under arrest, he was told to spread his legs and extend his arms to his side and Officer Kasey began his search. He searched Denzel's upper body first, and as he was about to search his lower body, Denzel spun around and pushed Officer Kasey away from him. He tried to run, but Officer Kasey was too quick and tackled him to the ground, at which point he handcuffed him. After bringing Denzel to his feet, he continued to search his person and found a loaded .25 caliber semi-automatic handgun that Officer Kasey seized and secured. The officer then gathered the remaining evidence for submission as part of the criminal case.

7 When Mr. Sears got back to his office, he found that the other APs had collected statements from Jerry and Ronald, and they had searched each boy's person and found bags of up to three ounces of marijuana, along with marijuana rolling papers and a few hundred dollars on each boy. These boys were held in the APs' office until Officer Kasey could take them into police custody. When the APs searched the boy's

lockers, they found nothing, but when they searched Ronald's car, which was in the student parking lot, they found a loaded gun and two switchblades, which at that time were "prohibited weapons" in the state penal code.

All three boys were arrested, and the APs immediately contacted CHS Principal Kate Austin to brief her on the situation. They then prepared their expulsion paperwork for each boy, which would be a placement at the Juvenile Justice Disciplinary Alternative Educational Program (JJAEP), if not in Jail. Each of the suspect's parents was called and told of their son's searches and seizures, what was found, and the arrest, which all of them already knew about because they were contacted by an SRO. Finally, the APs invited them to the discipline hearing for their sons, and they explained that because the boys were arrested on felony charges, an expulsion would be recommended at the hearing.

Two days later, each boy had his own separate hearing: The first hearing was at the campus level with the principal, and the second hearing was at the district level with the hearing officer. The parents of Jerry and Ronald refused to come to the school, as their sons were still in juvenile detention. They told the administrators that they could do whatever they thought they needed to do and that they would not complain. Therefore, at the campus hearing, the principal upheld AP Sears's recommendation to expel Jerry and Ronald to the JJAEP for a minimum of one year. When Mr. Sears went to the district hearing, his recommendation was also upheld, and both Jerry and Ronald would be expelled for one year at the JJAEP.

At his discipline hearing, Denzel was not present as he was still in jail, but his parents showed up with a lawyer. Before the meeting could start, the lawyer served the principal, Mr. Sears, and Officer Kasey with court documents that stated they were being sued for violations of civil liberties. They also refused to stay for the hearing as they were sure Denzel would be out of jail in a matter of days and would be seen as innocent.

Principal Austin told them it was their choice to leave or stay for the campus-level hearing, but either way, the hearing would be held and, because drugs and weapons were found during the search, the recommendation would be expulsion for one year. Furthermore, as Denzel is eighteen years old and was arrested as an adult, he could spend his expulsion time in jail. It was explained that a teacher from the district would go to the jail to teach him his core courses, so that he would still have access to his education. The parents and their lawyer walked away as Mrs. Austin was trying to finish her last sentence.

After Denzel's parents and their lawyer left the principal's office, Mrs. Austin, Mr. Sears, and Officer Kasey came together to call the superintendent and Chief O'Kelley. They would need guidance from both of them and the district lawyer on what steps to take for the allegations of violating Denzel's rights, which read,

- Each named defendant has violated Denzel's Fourth Amendment rights by searching and seizing without his or his parent's permission, which means that anything found during that search cannot be used as evidence. Additionally, the lawsuit listed that Denzel's Fourth Amendment right was violated further because Officer Kasey completed the search and seizure without a warrant.
- Each named defendant violated Denzel's Fourth and Fourteenth Amendment rights by violating his privacy in searching his locker and person without permission or explanation and in a school hallway where onlookers could see what was occurring.
- Each named defendant violated Denzel's Fourteenth Amendment rights by not equally protecting him because of his black skin color and automatically thinking the worst of him without provocation. Additionally, a violation of Denzel's due process rights occurred as Denzel was never given a chance to hear any allegations or to refute the allegation. Finally, according to Denzel, Officer Kasey never provided Denzel his Miranda Rights when he was arrested.

As Superintendent Littleton and Chief O'Kelley were listening to the conference call from Mrs. Austin, Mr. Sears, and Officer Kasey, the superintendent's secretary handed him a note that he and the Chief were about to be served by the same lawyer's messenger who was in the reception area. The documents showed that Denzel was suing the superintendent, the Chief, and the school board for violating his Fourteenth Amendment rights by allowing, through policy, Principal Austin, AP Sears, and Officer Kasey to harass, search, seize, and slander his name without provocation or reason. Dr. Littleton told Mrs. Austin, Mr. Sears, and Officer Kasey to meet the Chief and him after school so that all of them could sit down with the school district lawyer(s) and discuss where they would go from here.

WHAT ELSE DO I NEED TO KNOW?

The following is a brief insight into the issues presented in the case study, with a brief literature review to help give context to those issues.

The Fourth and Fourteenth Amendments and Miranda Rights

As educators and SROs work with students, it is important to know what and how federal and state laws affect public schools. Federal law does have a place on the campus; in fact, many states have aligned their state constitutions and bill of rights to the federal Constitution and other laws. This means that it can be assumed that the state codes or statutes are also aligned to the federal law. For this case study, the two main federal laws that are important to know are the Fourth and the Fourteenth Amendments and the case law arising out of the *Miranda v. Arizona* supreme court case law. In the United States Constitution's Fourth Amendment, it is stated,

> The right of the people to be secure in their persons, houses, papers, and effects, against unreasonable searches and seizures, shall not be violated, and no warrants shall issue but upon probable cause, supported by oath or affirmation, and particularly describing the place to be searched, and the persons or things to be seized. (U.S. Const. amend. IV)

It essentially is referred to as the search-and-seizure amendment. Most states have a statute that reiterates the Fourth Amendment, and many school districts have a policy or rule that aligns to the state codes pertaining to searches and seizures at the school level. It is important that all educators and SROs on a campus understand search and seizure expectations. For example, some school districts only allow administrators to search a student and seize evidence on campus, whereas others relegate this duty to either the police or an administrator.

In the Fourteenth Amendment, two very important phrases are pertinent for school administrators to remember: due process and equal protection. Specifically, part of Section 1 of the Fourteenth Amendment reads, "nor shall any State deprive any person of life, liberty, or property, without due process of law; nor deny to any person within its jurisdiction the equal protection of the laws" (U.S. Const. amend. XIV § 1).

These phrases are what all educators, specifically administrators, must abide by when working with any person on a campus. When working with students, administrators must give due process, which means simply for an administrator to give a student a chance to tell his or her side of the story and to investigate and look for supporting evidence that will confirm or contradict that story. Equal protection is following federal, state, and local laws and enforcing them fairly and consistently for all.

The "Miranda Rights" dictated by the U.S. Supreme Court as a result of the 1966 U.S. Supreme Court case *Miranda v. Arizona* are used as a warning to a criminal suspect against self-incrimination and given by the police before an in-custody interrogation. A reasonable effort of the following must be given when a person is in police custody and is or is about to be questioned:

- You have the right to remain silent;
- anything you say can be used against you in a court of law;

- you have the right to an attorney and to have him present during questioning;
- if you cannot afford an attorney, one will be appointed for you by the proper court; and
- you have the right to terminate the interview at any time. (*Miranda v. Arizona* 1966)

The Miranda Rights do not have to be told to a person unless they are in custody; it exists to warn one that he/she is about to be questioned. If a person is under arrest for a crime and the officer is not going to question that person, there is no requirement of Miranda. However, some states or some city police departments can choose that the Miranda Rights will be read when anyone is arrested and/or questioned, but those are policies subject to administrative review by the agency, not the law.

Searches and Seizures

What is legal in schools when it comes to searches and seizures? Can any educator search and seize and can an SRO search and seize at will? Many different states have their own education codes that address searches and seizures in schools and most give educators the power to search and seize any student when a reasonable cause is gained. A search must be "justified at its inception and reasonable in scope" (Walsh, Kemerer, & Maniotis, 2014, 373). A warrant is not needed by school employees to conduct a search; however, it is imperative that state and district codes are followed and understood before enforcing a search. Because SROs are peace officers, they will not search anyone unless they have probable cause (reasonable grounds for making a search or making an arrest).

For instance, not all states and/or school districts allow all educators to conduct a search and a seizure. What may be approved by a state legislature and/or by a school board is that those who can conduct a search and seizure are administrators who are the designated disciplinarians of the campus. Some also designate that the campus crisis team may conduct a search, which would mean teachers on the team would be able to search and seize when a suspicion or reasonable belief has been gained. Always try to be diligent in gaining a reasonable cause to search and seize so that any legal action against you or your employer can be defended.

Many courts throughout the nation have heard and decided cases that deal with searches and seizures at schools. One of the most referenced school court cases comes from *New Jersey v. T.L.O.* The New Jersey Court made the following points in the majority opinion for educators to follow when searching and seizing, as outlined by Walsh, Kemerer, and Maniotis (2014):

- Establish reasonable cause for believing that the student is violating or has violated a student rule or a law, and
- ensure that the search is reasonable in scope in light of the age and sex of the student and the nature of the offense. (p. 366)

In short, school officials do have the responsibility to keep safety and order on school campuses and may, based on reasonable cause or reasonable belief, search a student who is violating or has violated the SCOC or criminal law. As with any other violation of the SCOC and/or law, a school official must always assess the violation in relation to the student's age, gender, and nature of the offense. In some states, students younger than the age of ten are exempt from certain consequences of the law because of their age.

For example, if a group of kindergarten boys are having a peeing contest in the bathroom and absentmindedly spray the walls as they relieve themselves, a consequence for this type of behavior may be that the boys clean up their mess and miss two recess days, along with a stern verbal reprimand. However, if this same incident occurred at the high school level, because of the expectations that high school students are held to because of their age, the consequences may be more severe and may include in-school suspension and a police ticket/citation.

Some court cases have upheld the ability of school officials to keep safety and order on a campus. In *Patman v. State of Georgia* (2000), Officer Dale Pope, from Clarke County Police Department on special detail, was informed by a secretary that a student smelled like marijuana. Officer Pope stopped Patnam, a student at Clarke Central High School, and immediately smelled "a strong odor of marijuana." Officer Pope then frisked Patnam and felt several packages of "little stamp bags" with which Pope was familiar as bags used to package marijuana. Because Patman smelled of marijuana, Pope believed Patman had marijuana in his pocket. When Officer Pope asked Patman what was in his pocket, Patman responded, "Pope, come on and let me slide." This statement was viewed as a confession, and Pope reached into Patman's pocket and found eight bags of marijuana. The court upheld the search and seizure, citing that Officer Pope had established that Patman smelled of marijuana, he felt the "little stamp bags," and Patman's statement gave probable cause for the search and seizure. If Patman was searched by school officials, all that would have been needed is a reasonable cause (also called reasonable suspicion), which would have been fulfilled by the secretary's observations and the strong marijuana odor coming from Patman.

In another case, *A. H. v State of Florida* (2003), a PE teacher, Matthew Koff, noticed that A. H.'s speech was slurred after asking several times for him to repeat and then spell his name. Koff, having no special training with children on drugs but educating himself by reading pamphlets in college, felt that something was not right with A. H. and went to the assistant principal (AP), whom he told that A. H. may be "on something." The assistant principal then called A. H. in, told him that he was suspected of taking something like drugs, and when A. H. stated he did not take anything, he was instructed to empty his pockets. The AP then opened A. H.'s wallet and found a bag of leafy green material and a razor blade .

The State did not uphold this search and seizure because there was not a reasonable belief that A. H. was "on something." The primary reason Koff reported A. H. to the AP was due to A. H.'s not being able to articulate his name so that Koff could understand. This does not justify as reasonable cause and, hence, the search and seizure was not upheld (*A. H., A Child, Appellant v. State of Florida*, 2003). Note that in this Florida case, if the AP had been able to articulate that Koff's observations were confirmed and that the AP's personal experiences of observing or dealing with persons under the influence of alcohol or drugs led him personally to believe that A. H. was indeed intoxicated, it may have been reasonable to investigate further.

What these cases illustrate is that the school official must ascertain a reasonable cause before a search and seizure can be performed. This means that a school official must have some sort of articulable information or evidence that will lead someone to believe that the student has something that is in violation of the SCOC and/or the penal statutes. Furthermore, when it comes to police officers and SROs on campuses, it is best not to involve them until the higher level of actable information and/or probable cause is present to search and/or seize a student. The SRO may observe you as you search a student as a witness, however. To be knowledgeable and current of SRO programs and the duties that SROs should be able to perform on a campus, check with your district policies and visit the links below.

- National Association of School Resources Officers (NASRO), http://www.nasro.org
- Community Oriented Policing Services http://www.cops.usdoj.gov/default.asp?Item=54
- The National School Shield http://www.nraschoolshield.com/index.html

Campus and District Hearings

One of the most important things for all educators, but especially administrators who discipline students is to study the SCOC, which should be viewed as the law of the land for your school district and campus (Trujillo-Jenks & Trujillo, 2013). Within the code, there are different sections that point to the different types of violations, such as expellable, serious, major, and minor violations. The different types of violations are described in each section and detail what is expected from an administrator when disciplining students.

When studying the SCOC, discipline administrators must understand what type of consequences may be given to students who violate the rules. They must also understand at what age an arrest may happen, when family court will be involved, or where students go when they are expelled. It is important to recognize how discipline is documented at the district level and how that documented information is sent to the state. Most important to understand is the number of days required by law to give a suspension, contact a parent in writing, and have a discipline hearing.

When it comes to discipline hearings, it would be good to know what violations of the SCOC would warrant a student's being placed in a disciplinary alternative education program (DAEP), which does include JJAEP. Understanding how discipline hearings work in your district is crucial, especially if there is more than one level of hearings needed to place a student in a DAEP. A DAEP is sometimes a separate campus on its own but may be on another campus, like a school within a school. The DAEP campus is for students who have been expelled or committed a serious violation of the SCOC and/or the penal code. DAEP is also for students who are persistent rule breakers and who have tallied multiple violations of the SCOC. A set time frame is set for the student to stay at DAEP before being allowed to make it back to campus.

For a student who is in special education, the campus hearing must start with a manifestation hearing, or LINK (connection) individualized educational plan (IEP) meeting. This meeting is the special education meeting that must determine the answers to two main questions per the Individuals with Disabilities and Educational Act (IDEA):

1 Was the conduct in question caused by, or had a direct and substantial relationship to, the child's disability; or
2 was the conduct in question the direct result of the local education agency's failure to implement the IEP. (Wright, 2006, pp. 11–12).

If the IEP committee's answer is "yes" to one or both of the questions above, the student will have a behavior intervention plan developed. Also, the committee can decide what is in the best interest of the student: leave him or her on campus with stricter consequences or allow the recommendation to DAEP to be heard. Additionally, if the student has been arrested for both a penal code and SCOC violation, such as bringing a weapon on campus, the student will automatically go to DAEP, as that would be considered an expellable offense, even if "yes" is the answer to both questions. If the IEP committee answers "no" to both questions, the hearing will continue as it would for a general education student.

Document, document, document when dealing with student discipline. Be prepared to defend how you proceed with a student, specifically the consequences that are given for a violation of the SCOC. This defense will be documented in your notes, student and educator statements, physical evidence, and anything else that will help to support your decision. Additionally, campus and district hearings can be stressful, so be sure to follow your school district policies, and always have all data needed to make a sound decision. Understanding how a manifestation determination meeting should occur will also help you to have a smoother hearing. As Dwyer (1997) stated, "There is nothing in IDEA that restricts schools from disciplining children with disabilities. In fact, some would say that, by not addressing these dangerous behaviors, the student with special needs is not receiving an 'appropriate' education" (paragraph 4).

NCZ—NO CONSEQUENCE ZONE

Answer the questions below by applying what you know about this case and thinking about the steps you would take if you were faced with this situation or a similar one.

1 Unfortunately, discipline in schools encompasses everything from tardiness, to mutual fighting, to murder because some students are bold in breaking the law while on campus. List the different discipline issues that are occurring on your campus and assess how the educators are working on decreasing these issues.

2 Crime Stopper Hotlines have been implemented on many campuses across the nation.
   a. Do you have such a tip line, and what kinds of reasonable cause must you have before you move forward on disciplining a student, according to your state and district codes and policies?
   b. What does your SRO need to do or know to pursue a tip received from the hotline?
   c. How could the administrators and SROs have avoided the lawsuit in the case study?
   d. Is there anything that you would have done differently?

3 The SRO is an excellent resource and backup for administrators and all educators. Understanding their role and what is expected of them will help educators to perform their duties ethically and according to the law.
   a. What are your school district's expectations and guidelines for SRO?

   b. What are the specifics listed in your school's policies and in the SCOC concerning search and seizures?
   c. What is the administrator's role, and what is the SROs role in search and seizures?
   d. What are the ramifications of an administrator who does not fully understand the purpose or duties of an SRO on a campus?
4 Discipline hearings can be emotional and tense, especially for parents who believe their child has been targeted unfairly. Discipline hearings are used as the last resort, usually when a recommendation for placing a student in a DAEP is being discussed.
   a. Find the mandatory violations and expellable violations in your SCOC.
   b. Discuss what it means to expel a student from your campus: Where does the student go?
   c. What is needed for setting up and proceeding with a discipline hearing in your district, and discuss how it differs from the information presented in this case and in the *What Else Do I Need to Know* section.
   d. In some school districts, there are two levels for a student to be heard at a hearing: campus level and district level. How many levels does your district have, and what is the reason?
5 Looking at the big picture,
   a. what are the social ramifications for the two eighth graders specifically, and all eighth graders in that school district as a whole? Do eighth graders in your school district have an opportunity to earn high school credit at the high school?
   b. What needs to occur at the middle school and the high school to ensure the safety of those eighth graders attending class at the high school?

REFERENCES

Dwyer, K. (1997). Disciplining students with disabilities. *NASP Communique*, 26(2). http://www.nasponline.org/publications/cq262discipline.html

Trujillo-Jenks, L., & Trujillo, M. (2013). *The survival guide for new campus administrators: How to become a professional, effective, and successful administrator.* Austin, TX: Park Place Publications.

U.S. Const. amend. IV

U.S. Const. amend. XIV § 1

Walsh, J., Kemerer, F., & Maniotis, L. (2014). *The educator's guide to Texas school law* (8th ed.). Austin, TX: University of Texas Press.

Wright, P. W. D. (2006). IDEA 2004 regulations part E: Procedural safeguards. http://www.wrightslaw.com/idea/law/idea.regs.subparte.pdf

Chapter 11

The Jealous Shooter

Safety, order, and civility: These are the cornerstones of a healthy campus, and each of us knows what it is when we see it. Districts should be sure to define how safety, order, and civility can be maintained on their campuses, and administrators should be consistent in their attempts to ensure that each person who sets foot on the campus adheres to rules designed to keep the campus safe, orderly, and civil. The safety of students and educators on a campus is a large responsibility for any educator but of particular interest of the campus administrators and especially the school resource officers (SROs).

However, how do educators work through a situation where a person on campus decides to violate the sacred safety, order, and civility of a campus? What rules, policies, or laws are in place to help educators and SROs to protect a campus from unlawful and criminal acts? What should educators do when the unlawful act comes from a student? The following case focuses on a relationship between two students that has deteriorated. This relationship becomes a disaster.

THE CASE

Basketball season is always full of excitement at Ortega High School (OHS) because both the boy's and girl's basketball teams are in the playoffs for the state champions. Both teams have been the state champions for the past two years. Every game has been sold out this year, and the teams have proven to be worth the money that fans have spent. The fans are very enthusiastic yellers and chanters and also courteous and gracious winners, so no real drama occurs that the assistant principals and SROs at OHS could not handle. This makes OHS a great place to work and a place that is the first choice for many educators across the school district to vie to transfer to each year.

Becca Loves Carter

Becca and Carter are Ortega's favorite couple. They are both seniors, and both are captains of their varsity basketball team. Different university basketball scouts have approached both, and Carter has already signed with a Division 1 university in the south, as have a few of his teammates. Becca is waiting for the same university to ask her to play basketball for the ladies' team in hopes she can stay with Carter. Two Division 2 universities have approached her, but they are both in the northeast part of the country, and Becca is not showing interest.

Since eighth grade, Becca and Carter have been together as a couple. They are good students, with good attitudes and respectful demeanors. The teachers voted them best behaved in class, and their classmates voted them best couple and most likely to succeed. They are popular kids with many friends and admirers, and just about everyone thinks they are the perfect couple. Even their families are excited about Becca and Carter being together, and they are looking forward to one day becoming in-laws.

Sadly, things are no longer as they were in eighth grade. Although Becca and Carter would agree that they are in love, Carter is feeling a bit suffocated lately. Just recently, Becca began constantly badgering Carter about who he hangs out with and where he goes when he is not with her. Because of this jealous behavior, he has had doubts about continuing his relationship with Becca. Additionally, he has been very excited at the prospect of leaving home and going to another state to go to school, especially since Becca has become obsessed with getting accepted to the same university as he. He has secretly hoped that Becca does not get an offer to the school he wants to attend, and he has been slowly working up the courage to break up with Becca before graduation.

Shortly after their senior year started, Becca had become fixated on her relationship with Carter. The defining moment for this obsession occurred during a pre-senior summer party where other students from other high schools attended. Some girls from other high schools were seen flirting with Carter, and this incensed Becca. Carter liked the attention but made it clear that he had a girlfriend whom he loved very much. Nonetheless, Becca became insecure, obsessed, and scared of losing Carter to another girl and made a scene by yelling to everyone that Carter and she were going to get married and have children together. She continued by saying that "any girl who comes near Carter will get hurt!" This declaration embarrassed and angered Carter to the point that he left the party without Becca, and went home.

Lately, Becca has voiced to anyone who would listen that her priorities for her future depended on Carter. She plans to go to the same university Carter goes to, and even if she is not accepted or does not receive a scholarship, she plans to go to a community college near the university until she is accepted. Her dreams also include putting earning a basketball scholarship behind her and concentrating on making Carter happy. This revelation has scared Carter because he feels Becca was putting too much pressure on him to commit to a life that he had not given as much thought to; all he wants to do is play basketball at a top university and earn a degree. All the serious parts of life would come later.

These days, Becca has become clingier and more demanding of Carter's time, so much so that she expects that he text or call her about each move he makes throughout the day. Carter, once an outgoing, vivacious, and gregarious student, has become nervous, anxious, and neglectful of his grades. This new demeanor has brought on a hardened and aloof Carter, which has worried his parents and some of his teachers, but none thought his behavior was really something to be concerned about.

He really started to feel overwhelmed with Becca when she began a midnight ritual where she called him on his cell, woke him from his sleep, and hurled questions, asking, "*WHERE HAVE YOU BEEN? WHO HAVE YOU BEEN WITH?*" After a usual hour of calming her down, Carter would then try to go back to sleep but found himself watching TV until school started. This routine deprived Carter of a good night's sleep and contributed to his current and unusual lack of success in his classes.

During the school day, Becca would constantly text Carter to tell him where to meet her after class or to tell him what their daily schedule would entail. If Carter did not answer a text, Becca would come barreling through a classroom to see whether Carter was in class, which he always was. The teachers never thought much of this act, because their minds were occupied with preparing their students for the upcoming state testing. Although this embarrassed Carter, he never made a big deal about it to Becca, but when their friends started making comments and asking questions about the viability of their relationship past graduation, he knew others noticed what he thought was just his sometimes overactive imagination: the deterioration of their relationship. Additionally, he would make excuses not to eat with her during lunch, and he began to dodge her whenever he saw her in the hallway, which prompted their friends to question how their senior year and relationship would end.

As the perfect couple's relationship had become strained, Carter felt the need to make a clean break from Becca before graduation. Although he would have liked to wait until after prom, he worried that he would not be able to be civil to Becca if he waited any longer. Even though he hoped that Becca would break up with him, especially since he had been ignoring her phone calls and slowly avoiding her after school hours, he knew that he would need to put an end to this dying relationship. He felt terrible for feeling so trapped by the person that he still loved, but he just could not live like this anymore.

Therefore, he chose to break up with Becca in early March, a very busy and stressful month, when both the boys' and girls' teams had done so well during their regular basketball season that they were in the playoffs to determine whether they would make it to the state tournament. He just could not put up with the obsessive behavior anymore, so on a Thursday evening, he texted Becca asking whether she would meet him the next morning before he boarded the bus to travel to the playoff game. Becca immediately called when she received the text, but Carter ignored the call. He then had the following texting conversation with Becca.

Carter	Becca
Can we meet tomorrow before I get on the bus?	Why aren't U answering your phone?!!!?????!!!!????!
Can we meet tomorrow before I get on the bus for the game?	I'll come over right now. I LOVE YOU!!!!!xoxoxoxo
BECCA, answer my question and don't come over.	What is wrong with U? Why R U treating me like this? Do you love someone else??!?!!!?!?!
Becca, we need to talk and I wanna meet with you tomorrow before I go to the game.	I want 2 talk 2. We have so much to plan about our future 2gether. We will be so happy. xoxoxoxox I LOVE YOU!!!!!!!!
I wanna talk about our future too. How about we talk before I leave for the game?	Just talk to me NOW!!!!!
I'll see you tomorrow at school.	I'm going to call you NOW!!! ANSWER YOUR DAMN PHONE!!!

Becca called Carter twenty-three times, but Carter turned off his phone and walked out of his room. When he returned two hours later, he found twenty-three messages with varying degrees of hysteria. In one message she yelled,

I will kill myself if you don't pick up!!!!!!

In another message, she cried,

> I know you hate me and you don't want me anymore. I'll leave you alone, but I want you to always know that I will always love you, forever!

Still, in another message, she steadily stated,

> You better not dump me! Who do you think you are?! You took my virginity and now you think it is okay to DUMP ME? I will show you! You will regret ever hurting me, you &%$#!

And, last, she cried,

> I love you Carter, I love you!!!!! Don't you know how much I love you?!!! I will do anything, anything, just don't ever leave me, pleeeaaassseee!

Hearing this last message, Carter felt compassion and called Becca. When she picked up, she was still crying and immediately reiterated her love and devotion. He replied,

> I'm sorry, Becca, but I just can't go on like this anymore. I love you, too, but we can't be together any longer.

Becca cried and cried and begged Carter not to break up with her. After several minutes, Carter told Becca that he would always remember her kindly as she was his first love. He then hung up. Becca cried all night, feeling hopeless, helpless, and confused. She could not sleep and did not know what she was going to do.

The Big Game

It was the day of the game that would determine whether OHS would go to the State Tournament. This game was scheduled to be in a city about an hour away, so there was a morning pep rally scheduled that would continue until the boys boarded the bus and left school grounds. The pep rally attracted the students, teachers, parents, and community members. The other high schools in the district allowed their basketball players to go to OHS to help cheer on the OHS boys, and the feeder schools (middle and elementary schools) transported the older students to join the pep rally. The school gyms, hallways, and outside parking lot were full of fans, which made the start of the playoff game day fun and exciting for the members of the boys' basketball team.

Carter was keyed up, but he was a bit groggy from not getting enough sleep last night; however, he felt good for the first time in months and he knew that he would rise to the occasion and play a good game. He did notice that Becca was absent from the pep rally and decided that her absence was a good thing. He hoped that Becca would see that the breakup would be a positive for both of them, especially as a new chapter of their lives was about to start after graduation.

As the fans were filling the gym and hallways, the boys were on the court shooting hoops. Since OHS has more than 2,300 students, three of the five assistant principals were in the gym, while the principal and the associate principal were outside in the parking lot. Two assistant principals, Mr. Bill Nimitz and Mrs. Liza Robinson, were in the hallway. OHS has two SROs assigned to the campus, Officer Katie Friend and Officer Leo Petty, who were also in the hallway. The SROs notified the city police department about the pep rally and asked that they have officers nearby to help with traffic coming onto and going off the campus.

Before the pep rally started, the boys came off the court and went into their locker room. Mr. Nimitz and Officer Friend moved to their station at the entrance of the gym, while Mrs. Robinson and Officer Petty moved a few feet away in the concession/hall area near the locker rooms.

Because the pep rally was about to start, the principal and associate principal came back inside. The principal started the pep rally with the Pledge of Allegiance and then welcomed the community members and the visiting students from the other schools. Some special guests were OHS's namesake, Command Sergeant Major Stephen Ortega, a prominent Vietnam veteran who was a community hero; the town's mayor; the superintendent; three school board members; and four city council members. She also reminded the students of the expected behaviors and courtesies of pep rally decorum, which led to the cheerleaders' taking over with a cheer that brought the entire gym and hallway to their feet chanting, "STATE, STATE, STATE!" The cheer was supposed to be the signal for coach Bonhiem to bring the boys out of the locker room and into the gym, but after about two minutes, no boys' team emerged. Everyone just thought that coach Bonhiem had some last minute things to say to his winning team and just kept cheering until the boys were seen.

Suddenly, a gunshot was heard, then another, and finally a third shot was heard from the boys' locker room. The crowd in the hallway near the locker room began to scream and started to run outside. Most of the crowd that was in the gym heard the screaming and did not know what was happening, as the crowd was so loud, and the gunshots were not heard by everyone. However, as those fans closest to the hallway began to understand that it was gunshots that were heard, they began to run out of the gym. Because the gym was beyond capacity, the administrators tried to guide everyone in an orderly fashion to the doors. Their biggest fear, at this time, was how to help those students in wheelchairs and with ambulatory health issues to get to safety. Still, there were some elementary teachers who told their students to hide and crouch under the bleachers because they knew the crowd leaving the gym in panic could crush them.

Simultaneously, in the hallway, Officer Friend looked at Mr. Nimitz and nodded that she was going toward the gunshots. Officer Petty was near the locker room, so he went in first where the gunshots came from and, at the same time, he was radioing the city dispatch, "Shots fired at Ortega! Shots fired at Ortega, send more units!" Officer Friend reached the boy's locker room and followed Officer Petty's lead. In a two-officer stack, they would enter the locker room from the front door. Officer Friend radioed for the responding units to cover the locker room's outside door. At the same time, Mrs. Robinson and Mr. Nimitz were trying to usher people either outside or back into the gym from the hall/concession/area. There was much chaos, but the hall/concession area quickly became bare in a matter of minutes as the fans ran screaming outside. As the last person seemed to be out of the door, the APs locked all doors and stood near the boys' locker room as they radioed the principal and other administrators about what had happened.

Outside, the city police officers who were arriving directed the crowd to pass them, trying to ensure that the armed officers were between the shooter(s) and the innocents. As more officers arrived, an inner perimeter was set up outside all exits from the gym/locker room area. As more and more units arrived, groups of four officers began to stack together to enter the building and find the source of the gunfire.

In the locker room, Officer Petty and Officer Friend made quick entry and assessed the situation by asking those present, "Where's the shooter?!" Coach Bonheim advised that he was kneeling on top of her: Becca, was face down on the ground with her hands being held behind her back. They saw that a boy (Carter) was on the ground with visible wounds to the chest and stomach and that the school's athletic trainers were at Carter's side giving him first aid. Officer Petty radioed for paramedic response and notified all police units that the shooter was disarmed and in custody as Officer Friend placed handcuffs on Becca and searched her for any other weapons. Coach Elliott, the assistant basketball coach, had been shot in the shoulder and was sitting in front of Becca on a locker room bench. The players were spread out and standing out of the way, as they saw both their teammate and Coach Elliott being attended to by the athletic trainers. The two SROs asked whether everyone else was okay, swept the rest of the room to ensure no other shooter was present, and began to gather information. They were able to ascertain the following:

1   About ten minutes before the pep rally and as the boys came back into the locker room from warming up, they sat to hear a pep talk from Coach Bonhiem. As they and the other coaches were settling down to

hear the words of wisdom, they saw Becca emerge from the bathroom stalls. She held a gun pointed out, and she quickly ran up to Carter and shot him once in the chest and, as Carter fell, she shot him again in the stomach.

2 As Becca was shooting Carter, Coach Elliott ran up to her, as did some of the players. Becca shot for the third time, striking Coach Elliot in his shoulder.

3 From behind, Coach Bonhiem tackled Becca and wrestled the gun from her, and some of the boys joined their coach and helped place Becca's hands behind her back. They tied her hands with a jump rope they use for warmups. Coach Bonhiem took possession of Becca's gun at this point.

4 The athletic trainers and other coaches ran to both Carter and Coach Elliott to help stop the bleeding and determine the seriousness of the wounds. They quickly surmised that Carter was dead and that Coach Elliott would be okay if he was taken to a hospital ASAP. Becca was not making any sounds as she continued to lie prostrate with her hands tied behind her back.

5 All the boys and the coaches were accounted for, and all were uninjured.

During this time, the city police and the Special Weapons and Tactics team were on site and swept and secured the premises. Some of the city police helped the APs get everyone out of the building and safely off campus. The city's chief of police joined the principal and superintendent on the scene. First responders were directed to set up a triage site and helped the principal and superintendent guide the parents of the Ortega basketball team to find their sons. The hardest job facing them would be to tell Carter's parents what had happened. Someone would have to call Becca's parents and ask that they meet the police officers at the police department. Who's job is it going to be to talk to the families, community, and media and how does OHS get back to normal? The administration and SROs were facing a daunting aftermath.

WHAT ELSE DO I NEED TO KNOW?

Crisis Plan

The ideal school will have no traumatic events or crises. Because there is no such utopia, preparing students and staff for a crisis is warranted. Additionally, because not all crises occur on campus, it is necessary for a school to create a plan for crises that may occur on and off campus: "Consequently, a school crisis plan should include protocols on how to handle emergency situations that occur in the community, both on and off school grounds" (Asprianti, Pelchar, Taylor, McCleary, Bain, & Foster, 2011, p. 147). Through the *3 Dos* of developing a crisis plan—*preparation, awareness, and enforcement*—crises can be lessened and possibly avoided (Trujillo-Jenks & Trujillo, 2013).

Being *prepared* is actively discussing with your colleagues what types of crises plans should be developed for your campus (Trujillo-Jenks & Trujillo, 2013). If your school is situated in a tornado area, a crisis plan for tornadoes should be developed. Because school shootings are not the only crisis that can reach the school doorstep, some schools have taken precautions against natural disasters and have had safe-rooms built within the schools. After the devastating tornado that hit Moore, Oklahoma, schools in Oklahoma are investing in safe rooms, which would be used for other school functions when not being used as a safe room (Kennedy, 2013).

In preparing to decide what type of crisis may happen on your campus, the Cole, Orsuwan, and Ah Sam research, which focused on college campuses, suggested that there are thirteen man-made disaster event categories applicable to college campuses: "sexual assault, stalking, campus dating violence, hate crimes, hazing, celebratory violence (riots), attempted suicides, suicides, murder/suicides, manslaughter, aggravated assault, arson, and attack on faculty and staff" (as cited in Booker, 2014, p. 17). Some of these man-made disasters have been seen at the public school level, and crisis plans to address some of these would be reasonable. According to Estep (2013), a comprehensive plan might also include responses to

- armed intruders,
- bomb threats,
- severe weather,
- death of a student/staff,
- loss of power or phone service,
- child abuse,
- fire,
- hostage situations,
- possession or use of firearms or other weapons,
- chemical, gas, or biological contamination,
- terrorist activities, and
- pandemic. (p. 14)

Hence, crises plans should align with the needs of the school and should include short-and long-term goals and strategies that "can be adjusted in response to any contingency" (Regan, 2014, p. 52). For this reason, it is essential that each school has a team that responds during the crisis and follows a prescribed plan outlining actions that address most, if not all, possible crisis situations.

Specifically, when it comes to school shootings, it is good to note that "School shootings are most commonly committed by either a student who goes to the school or by an intruder from off campus who has a connection to someone within a particular school" (Duplechain & Morris, 2014, p. 145). Additionally, the statistics that illuminate school shootings are alarming. From their research on school shootings from 1760 to 2010, Duplechain and Morris (2014) found the following:

> It is worth noting that America has witnessed four major school shootings in recent years... Since 2010, there have been at least 80 more school shootings. That's an average of 20 school shootings per year from 2010 to 2014. (p. 145)

They further assert that the most common behaviors or factors of school shootings that many educators may see on a daily basis are bullying, lack of parental involvement or presence at school or at home, and the lack of maturity to deal with serious matters (p. 144–148). The authors also suggest that a school shooter profile be created; one that focuses on behaviors that students display.

Awareness is knowing how the campus is arranged, who has access to the campus, what academic or sponsored activities teachers do outside the classroom, and what identified areas on campus are concerns for high probability of Student Code of Conduct (SCOC) violations (Trujillo-Jenks & Trujillo, 2013). Having working cameras on campus, some kind of security system where visitors to the campus are guided to the front office first, and keeping the staff aware of the expectations for being aware are all necessary. Also, all should note the following:

- Be aware of how those on your campus are behaving and, if any behaviors have changed, from one day to the next, report and/or investigate why;
- Be aware and recognize that some student work, like journals, essays, and drawings, may be anticipatory of a lethal situation; never dismiss a student's work, especially if graphic and/or specific details (or names) are discussed on how to murder others.
- Be aware of a system of knowing who is on your campus, like issuing school IDs to all who are students or staff members; have IDs made for parent volunteers and visitors, so that the IDs become the focal identifier for who should or should not be on the campus.
- Be aware of one's surroundings at all times, and report and/or investigate any unusual circumstances or events including alterations made to a building or other school property.

Being aware will help all educators on a campus become ever more vigilant in keeping a crisis abated.

The third *Do* is the *enforcement* of rules and policies and the development of crises plans (Trujillo-Jenks & Trujillo, 2013). Working with the staff in helping them to enforce the crisis plans through workshops or faculty meetings devoted to learning about the plans is necessary, and communicating the reason for certain crisis plans is essential. Schools must develop a crisis plan through a crisis team that is proactive and that provides professional development that shows how to respond to a crisis (Kennedy-Paine, Reeves, & Brock, 2013). Finally, enforcing them uniformly and consistently is a must.

After the *3 Dos* are met, Trujillo-Jenks and Trujillo (2013) also suggested that implementing and practicing the plan will help educators to find whether the plan does work, which would lead to reviewing and revising those elements that just did not work and reteaching the plan, striving for the best possible outcome.

Another way to create crisis plans is through The Safe and Sound: A Sandy Hook Initiative, which focuses on helping schools to become safer for all students and teachers through collaboration, sharing of information, and education (Gay, 2014). Through a visual called the "Safety Umbrella," many safety topics concerning safety can be addressed: fire safety, bus safety, environmental safety, security, health, and wellness (Gay, p. 22). These safety topics can be defined by an individual campus with possible safety concerns that are unique to that campus. Further, once these safety concerns are identified, Gay (2012) proposes that the Straight "A" Safety Model of assess, act, and audit be put in place.

All students on a campus must be considered when creating a crisis plan. This includes students with disabilities; educators must consider "the diverse range of intellectual, social, emotional, and physical development among children with disabilities" (Clarke, Embury, Jones, & Yssel, 2014, p. 170). Furthermore, Clarke et al. encourage educators to develop appropriate IEPs that focus on the specific and individual needs of a student during a crisis (i.e., medical condition, psychological condition, intellectual comprehension of the situation).

Crises will occur on campuses. Preparing for as many variables before the crises occur may help to prevent or lessen the damage of a crisis. Specifically, when implementing and practicing an active shooter crisis plan, the easiest and most prolific phrase that is a tip from *Ready Houston* (a project funded through a grant from the Department of Homeland Security) is "*Run, hide, fight.*" *Run* to escape and seek safety; *hide* if you cannot escape, and call for help, lock the door, and take shelter until safety comes; and *fight* as a last resort to stay alive. If nothing else is remembered, remind all on a campus of this simple phrase: "*Run, hide, fight.*"

For more specific information and access to *Ready Houston* visit http://www.readyhoustontx.gov/schoolready/index.html

For other information on active shooters and *"Run, hide, fight,"* visit http://www.fbi.gov/about-us/cirg/active-shooter-and-mass-casualty-incidents/run-hide-fight-video

Dealing with the Afterward

What happens after a crisis is just as important as what happens before and during. As many may want life to go on as it had before the crisis, some may have a difficult time getting back to "normal." One area of concern is the well-being of every person who experienced the crisis or traumatic event. Asprianti et al. (2011) confirmed that

> The main concern both during and after a crisis incident is the students' physical safety and mental well-being...It is important that school administrators realize that even a tragic event that occurs outside school premises has the potential to adversely affect students. (p. 147)

The well-being of students and staff after a crisis becomes a priority, and a plan of action should be included in the crisis plan to address how those on a campus will be helped.

Additionally, the mental health implications that become most evident after a tragedy should be considered. The psychological reactions associated with the aftermath of a crisis are usually deep and complex, which make it difficult for educators to identify (Cowan & Rossen, 2013). Some will experience and show overt signs of dealing with a crisis right away, while others may not until weeks or months later. As each person deals with traumatic events differently, it is not possible to know how to react to each individual. However, understanding that each individual connected to a crisis will experience some sort of emotional and mental breakdown will help those educators in the position to do so help to work in making the daily life of a school continue (Kennedy-Paine et al., 2013).

Some specific symptoms that may occur with students, specifically children having a difficult time coping with a crisis or traumatic event, could be

- fear of separation or clinging behavior;
- eating or sleeping problems;
- headaches or stomachaches;
- prolonged sadness;
- behavior problems;
- startled reactions to loud noises;
- acting younger than their age;
- fear of tragedy being repeated;

- withdrawal; and
- decline in academic performance. (Kennedy-Paine et al. 2013, p. 42)

Demaria and Schonfeld (2013) developed a similar list that focused on how children react and behave differently than adults. Depending on their development stage, cognitive capacity, and ability at managing high levels of stress and anxiety, students may also react according to the list below:

- anxiety, worries, and fears due to limited knowledge or experience and the tendency toward misunderstanding and misattribution;
- bereavement and grief if deaths resulted from the event;
- avoidance, withdrawal, and isolation;
- irritability, or angry outbursts; and
- somatization: developing physical health symptoms as a result of stress. (p. 13–14)

Although these lists identified symptoms for students, adults on a campus could also react in the same way and present like issues.

When dealing with a death on a campus, Garran (2013), speaking from the perspective of a principal who has seen many school deaths on his campus, provides a road map for educators. The abbreviated road map, shown below, includes the following elements:

1 initial notification and early communication;
2 activating the crisis leadership team;
3 social media as a friend;
4 negotiating the way forward;
5 funeral notification and attendance; and
6 after the funeral. (pp. 18–22)

This partial list of how to deal with a death on campus focuses on communication at many stages. This communication can take many forms, but what is most important to remember is to talk candidly with the students and staff about the tragedy, and use social media to your advantage (Duran, 2014). Social media can be used to update students, staff, and families quickly and may help quash rumors.

Preparing and dealing with the afterward of a crisis takes a lot of time and energy. For those tragedies that occur off campus, have a crisis plan ready that prepares educators to help students and other educators to get back to normalcy as quickly as possible. Educators should never forget that "Whether through acts of mass terrorism, destructive natural disasters, or isolated school shootings, high-profile events bring a renewed recognition that while schools as a whole are incredibly safe places, the unthinkable will happen somewhere at some point" (Cowan & Rossen, 2013, p. 9). Hence, safety, order, and civility on a campus are the cornerstones that should be cultivated daily.

NCZ—NO CONSEQUENCE ZONE

Answer the questions below by applying what you know about this case and thinking about the steps you would take if you were faced with this situation or a similar one.

1 Crisis plans are required on every campus. They are guides toward helping educators to work through different types of traumatic events.
   a. What types of crisis plans are in place at your school? Who should put these plans together? A crisis team?
   b. When it comes to crisis plans and keeping safety, order, and civility on a campus, what is your state's expectation?
   c. If your campus has gone through a crisis, what did you learn and how are you better prepared for future crisis?
   d. Would you and your crisis team create a shooter profile? Why or why not?
2 SROs are gems on a campus because they are able to help in serious situations, such as a school shooting.
   a. Is there an SRO on your campus, and what are his or her duties? If you do not have an SRO on your campus, do you have one assigned to the campus?
   b. Does your school district have its own police department? If so, what is the purpose of this department, and how are schools protected? What is the relationship of the police department and the schools?
   c. If there is no district police department, how does the city police department help your school? Is there community policing and, if so, does your school invite the community officer to the campus? Why is this important to know?
   d. What type of communications and understanding is there between the school district and the city police department?
3 Planning for the afterward is just as important as creating a crisis plan.
   a. What steps are in place to help students and staff deal with the afterward of a crisis?
   b. What should be the role of the counselor(s) at your campus? How can they help in preventing a crisis? What should they do in helping after a crisis has occurred on or off campus?
4 Dealing with an active shooter and with any weapon on campus should be a part of any school's crisis plan. However, many schools do not think past the crisis plan to the afterward or picking up the pieces.

a. At what point should the school offer assistance to the family whose child has been gunned down at school? Describe and discuss the different types of assistance. What should happen after a stabbing? A bow and arrow shot? Acid thrown in a student's or educator's face?

b. Should the school offer any assistance to the assailant?

c. What state or federal law could be used against the school if Carter's or Becca's family wanted to sue the school? Explain.

d. What should be the plan to help the other students and teachers to carry on and move forward with their lives after an active shooter event has occurred on campus?

5 Some students may not know how to react or behave in certain situations, like during a breakup or any other traumatic event.

a. What is the role of the school, if any, for helping students work through certain life events?

b. What is the role of your counselor(s) at your campus in these types of situations?

c. What is the duty of educators on a campus when it comes to students' change in behavior? Should educators involve themselves in student-to-student disagreements, such as a breakup or a disagreement?

d. Identify what is available at your campus or within your community to help students in sensitive situations.

6 Looking at the big picture, what are the social, emotional, and political consequences

a. for Ortega High School students and educators?

b. For Carter's and Becca's families?

c. For the community as a whole?

REFERENCES

Aspiranti, K. B., Pelchar, T. K., McCLeary, D. F., Bain, S. K., & Foster, L. N. (2011). Development and reliability of the comprehensive crisis plan checklist, *Psychology in the Schools*, 48(2), 146–155.

Booker, L. Jr. (2014). Crisis management: Changing times for colleges. *Journal of College Admission*, 222, 16–23.

Clarke, L. S., Embury, D. C., Jones, R. E., & Yssel, N. (2014). Supporting students with disabilities during school crises: A teacher's guide. *Teaching Exceptional Children*, 46(6),169–178.

Cowan, K. C., & Rossen, E. (2013). Response to the unthinkable: School crisis response and recovery. *Phi Delta Kappan*, 95(4), 8–12.

Demaria, T., & Schonfeld, D. J. (2013). Do it now: Short-term responses to traumatic events. *Phi Delta Kappan*, 95(4), 13–17.

Duplechain, R., & Morris, R. (2014). School violence: Reported school shootings and making schools safer. *Education*, 135(2), 145–150.

Duran, G. (2014). School districts' role during off-campus tragedies. *Education Digest*, 80(1), 32–35.

Estep, S. (2013). Crisis planning: Building enduring school community relationships. *Delta Kappa Gamma Bulletin*, 79(3),13–20.

Garran, C. (2013). A death at school: What school leaders should do. *Phi Delta Kappan*, 95(4), 18–22.

Gay, M. (2014). School safety: Lessons after loss. *Techniques: Connecting Education & Careers*, 89(7), 20–25.

Kennedy, M. (2013). Seeking safer schools. *American School & University*, 85(10), 18–24.

Kennedy-Paine, C., Reeves, M. A., & Brock, S. E. (2013). How schools heal after a tragedy. *Phi Delta Kappan*, 95(4), 38–43.

Ready Houston. (2013). Run, hide, fight. http://www.readyhoustontx.gov/schoolready/index.html

Regan, M. (2014). A false sense of security: Managing the aftermath of a crisis is what the author calls a new normal for school communities. *Education Digest*, 79(5), 51–55.

Trujillo-Jenks, L., & Trujillo, M. (2013). *The survival guide for new campus administrators: How to become a professional, effective, and successful administrator*. Austin, TX: Park Place Publications.

Chapter 12

Mini Case Studies

Be proactive and make decisions based on evidence. This means seeking others' insight into a particular event and finding the answers to a question. The answers become the evidence that allows educators to make data-driven decisions. Through the gathering of the evidence, data-driven decision making becomes a professionally supported one. Martin (2011) stated that data, or evidence, allows for a "succinct and unemotional call for change and support" (p. 31). This succinct and unemotional action helps an educator to focus on the facts and not on elements that do not pertain to an event, and further allows gathered data to be transformed to usable knowledge (as cited in Mandinach, 2012, p. 73).

For teachers and leaders, evidence will mean different things. Nevertheless, what is necessary for educators on a campus to understand is how to interpret, understand, and broker these data for appropriate use (Goren, 2012). For teachers, when data are mentioned, they usually mean information that focuses on what is being done in the classroom. Teachers may look at assessment data to make instructional delivery decisions for individual students, for example. Their decisions are based on the evidence that they have obtained; therefore, if teachers have an understanding of how to use classroom data to make changes in the classroom that improve student success, that same understanding can be applied to other events, such as disciplining a student for a violation of the student code of conduct.

For leaders, the gathering of data, or evidence, is done for an array of reasons, such as improving teacher success, student academics, and safety procedures at the campus. Data can be overwhelming and may give a leader an excuse that he or she just does not have the time to look at the data and still be effective. Some leaders may even believe that data involve numbers only, which means that gathering evidence to answer a question that does not involve numbers is not appropriate. However, data are any information that can be gathered to help an educator to make a sound decision.

Usually, when educators must work through events that occur on a campus, a question is posed. Therefore, finding the answer to that question encourages evidence to be sought to answer the question. Suggested steps in finding that answer are the following:

1 After a question is brought to your attention, gather information.
2 The information, or data, should come from as many sources as possible.
3 Make a decision based on this information. If the sources conflict, make a professional judgment call based on the information gathered at that time.
4 Reflect on the decision(s) made and seek how improvement can be obtained.
5 Apply what has been learned to the next situation.

Regardless of what steps educators take in making data-driven decisions, continuously making decisions based on gathered information should become a natural and continued practice.

This chapter is for the educator on the go with nine topics presented with at least two mini-scenarios that focus on each topic. Discuss the variables presented in each mini-scenario, then using the information that is presented, discuss the following questions:

1 If this occurred on your campus, how would you handle this situation as a teacher/administrator? Name the steps you would take.
2 What codes/policies/rules/procedures/laws have been or may be violated through this scenario? Or, what codes/policies/rules/procedures/laws pertain to this scenario and what are possible consequences or outcomes?
3 How would you, as a teacher/administrator, prevent/consider this event if it occurred on your campus?
4 What information is still needed before you can make a data-driven decision?

These mini-scenarios are to help you to start thinking about possible events that may force you to think on your feet and to employ action that is necessary. Think about how these scenarios can help you learn more about the topic and its relationship to your campus. Enjoy learning and figuring out how to be a proactive educator.

CURRICULUM, INSTRUCTION, ATTENDANCE

1 A mother comes in to talk to you about her daughter's attendance record. She has a question about the difference between admissions and compulsory attendance. She would like to know what these mean, because she plans to take her daughter out of school for religious reasons. She explains that her daughter will miss up to fifteen days of school during each semester due to missionary work, and she wants them all excused.

2 A group of parents decide to home-school their children and use both online courses and courses that they will develop. They would like to know what the state codes and the school district polices are for home schooling. They would also like to borrow textbooks to use at home and would like to have their children attend elective courses at your campus, which is their community school. Finally, some of their children want to participate in sports at the high school level.

3 Frank turns eighteen next week and refuses to do any work because he tells you that once he is legally an adult, he is withdrawing himself and no longer will be attending school, which he believes complies with the state law. He, effectively, will become a dropout, and he tells you that there is nothing you can do about it. Frank also informs you that he can come back to high school whenever he chooses and demands that you give him information on the different possibilities of returning to public schools.

SPECIAL POPULATIONS

1 A mother just learned that her child is not eligible for special education services. According to the Full and Individual Evaluation (FIE), the child has the potential to learn, but as she chooses to skip school and has been a discipline problem (e.g., disruption in class, falling asleep in class, and truancy), the committee agreed with the report that she can be successful in the general education environment. The mother then asks you about 504 options, because now she wants her daughter to have 504 accommodations. She also wants an outside opinion and a new FIE that she demands the school pay for and provide. Finally, she wants her child to receive both 504 and special education services.

2 You are attending an individualized education plan (IEP) or an admission review and dismissal meeting as the general education teacher/administrator. The mother is very upset that her deaf/blind child has not made progress within the past year, even though the special education staff shows documented assessments and student work to prove the contrary. Nevertheless, the parent asks that you, the general education educator, help her convince the IEP team:

    a. to allow her child to not only have an intervener at school but at home at the expense of the school;

    b. to allow her to have a carte blanche pass that allows her to come and go on campus wherever and whenever she pleases, so that she can be assured that the school is following the IEP;

    c. to be notified daily of her daughter's progress, with a detailed explanation of what she has learned, what she did not understand, and what she has for homework, so that the mother can help her child at home (the mother has created a form she wants teachers to fill out); and

    d. to have detailed lesson plans submitted to her, at least one month in advance, so that she can help her daughter with her class work at home;

    e. to provide a tutor who will come to the house, at the school's expense, to help with homework.

3 A new family has moved to your school district, and they have eight children that will be attending your schools. All eight children have different learning needs, and the parents want to make sure that the school that each child will attend has the necessary curriculum and facilities for their children. They have children who will attend the elementary, middle, and high school nearest to their home; therefore, they plan to ask the following questions:

    a. What types of programs are available for our seventh grader who has childhood diabetes, and how will his teachers be notified of his conditions, without violating HIPPA? He was on a 504 plan at his last school; will he need to have a 504 plan at his new school?

    b. For our twin daughters who have IQs nearing 145 and who had a grade point average of 4.0 in their previous school, what type of classes are available that will challenge them? They are in the ninth grade.

    c. We have a son who loves to learn languages. He grew up learning English in our home, but he also speaks Spanish, French, and German. At present, he only speaks German at home and in public. What type of program will allow him to continue to speak German in all of his classes? Will he be able to take a type of class for English as a second language, but for German speakers? Is there a bilingual program for him at the elementary level, since he is in fourth grade?

    d. We have a rebellious son who plans to drop out of school when he turns age eighteen. He is sixteen now and has only two high school credits. He believes that if he only had a non-traditional school to attend, he could earn more credits. What type of non-traditional classrooms or schools do you have to offer our son?

e. The rest of our children are pretty normal, academically speaking. What types of courses or educational programs do you have to offer for our first grader, our third grader, and our eighth grader?

EDUCATOR CONTRACTS, ETHICS, AND ACADEMIC FREEDOM

1 Igotta Suue is a probationary teacher with a probationary contract on your campus. After several classroom observations by different administrators and a formal forty-five-minute evaluation/appraisal observation, Igotta was placed on a teacher growth plan in late January. The growth plan outlined the goals of what Igotta needed to accomplish, and it included the deficiencies that she needed to improve upon. She signed this contract and agreed to the terms, which basically stated that if she does not improve her deficiencies, she may have a non-renewed teaching contract at the end of the school year. A second formal forty-five-minute evaluation/appraisal observation was conducted in early March. Some improvement was made, but not all outlined goals were met; hence, her contract will not be renewed after this year. She has told her teacher buddies that she plans to get a lawyer and sue. She will bypass the grievance process, and she will win, as she believes that there is not enough evidence for non-renewal of her contract. She also stated that too many administrators were in her classroom observing her teaching, which made her classroom a hostile environment and that not all administrators agreed with her non-renewal status.

2 The Teacher Code of Ethics (TCoE) is posted in every classroom, in every workroom, and in every office on your campus. Working ethically and with integrity are important to the staff, and as reminders of performing their duties, notes with different ethical sayings are left in everyone's mailboxes or e-mailed at least once a week by the administration. With this known, a veteran teacher and a second-year teacher are overheard talking about a bilingual student, whom neither have in class as a student. As they are looking through cumulative folders, they find the one concerning the bilingual student. They gossip about the student's home life, talk about how close they live to the student, and how each will make a move on the very attractive father. They even read aloud the student's personal information, like the court documents that state that the father has full custody and the mother has relinquished rights to her child, but only a secretary and two passing teachers could hear the conversation.

3 A teacher is in his fifth successful year of teaching world history at a nearby high school. His colleagues, students, and the parents respect him and see him as an exceptional role model. He loves his job, and

his ability to teach controversial history topics with ease and grace has made his courses legendary. He also is a male stripper in a club across state lines. He has stripped for the last two years ever since his buddy told him of the easy and excessive money to be made. He strips only on weekends, his second job never interferes with his teaching duties, and he has not informed his school district of his second job. One evening, a group of women attend the strip club during a bachelorette party. One of the women is the mother of a student whom the teacher teaches and, on Monday morning, she reports the teacher's second job to the principal.

SPEECH RIGHTS OF EDUCATORS

1 Mr. Dude, is a biology teacher in the Happy School District and, in the biology book, there is a section on the human body's immune system with a corresponding unit on infectious diseases and their transmission. One disease presented in the unit is the acquired immune deficiency syndrome (AIDS). Mr. Dude thought it prudent and good teaching to show the class how to prevent sexually infectious diseases by placing a condom on correctly by using his finger in his demonstration. One student asked if one could still get pregnant "*even if the condom was on right.*" Mr. Dude said, "*Yes, but you need to talk to your parents for more elaboration.*" One student asked whether there were other ways to prevent pregnancies, while another asked whether there were other ways to have safe sex. The last question was one that concerned the purchase of the best and safest kinds of condoms. Mr. Dude told each student with a question to ask their parents their questions but that condoms could be bought almost anywhere. The bell rang, and as the students were leaving the classroom, several told Mr. Dude, "*Thank you for an exciting class.*" Another stated, "*This was the best information that I have learned all year.*" And another exclaimed, "*Now I know how to have safe sex.*"

2 Mrs. Teena loves getting on her Snapchat, Instagram, and Twitter pages, even while she is at school and in class. She is constantly posting pictures of herself and her students. She even brags about how smart her students are, how much they have learned throughout the school year from her, and how awesome her students' parents are for allowing her to post pictures of them on social media. Lately, she has been taking pictures of the school building and even included a picture of the school's marquee. She just loves her job and wants everyone to know it!

3 A terrible car wreck occurred early this morning that left a teacher dead and two students critically injured. The teacher has driven the two students to school each morning, as they all lived on the same street

and because the teacher and the students' parents were good friends. The news of the car wreck made it back to campus, and as you gather the staff to let them know what has occurred, you also tell them that no one should speak to the news stations and only the principal and superintendent's designee have permission to speak to all media. You also tell the staff that if any parent or student asks what happened, a written statement will be provided of the wreck and given to all staff to relay to the school community. One teacher believed that everyone should know what happened and that she had the right to speak to the media, so she sought them out during her lunchtime (which is her own time and she can do what she wishes) and tells them, "We were told not to speak to the media, but I believe that what has occurred to our school family is a community concern! I have the details of the car wreck, and I will answer all questions at this time."

STUDENT CODE OF CONDUCT

1 The valedictorian and senior class president went javelina hunting after school last Wednesday. The valedictorian missed Thursday and Friday because he was recovering from a sinus infection, so he forgot to remove all hunting gear from his truck. When he returned to school this week, the drug dogs were scheduled to search the student parking lot, and they hit on the valedictorian's car where a bow and arrow were found. This student has never been in trouble before, he is a likeable kid, is in all AP courses, and graduation is less than a month away. His mom is a state senator, and the boy was just appointed to the Air Force Academy.

2 A very explosive seventh grade student, Mary, has been sent to the assistant principal's office twelve times this year for numerous violations to the SCOC. She has demonstrated behaviors such as angry outbursts, profanity, hitting, and throwing objects, such as a chair and a laptop. Her victims have been both students and adults, and one student went to the hospital last week to get stitches after a laptop hit her forehead. The educators at the school have been working with the parents since they agreed to special education (SPED) testing and have worked with Mary to keep her on campus and not send her to the disciplinary alternative education program. However, when the time came to place Mary in a behavior management classroom because she qualified for services as a student with an emotional disability, her parents refused SPED services. Mary had another explosive situation occur today, where she cussed out the teacher and told him, *"I want to cut you up until you bleed!"*

3 A sixteen-year-old student who was intoxicated on Saturday night committed vehicular manslaughter after the car he was driving traveled

on the wrong side of the road and collided head-on with another car full of other teens who had been drinking. Two students from the other car were dead at the scene, and three students were taken by air ambulance to a hospital. The sixteen year-old student from your campus tried to flea the scene of the crash but was apprehended close by. The superintendent and principal discussed the situation and how to handle school on Monday morning, and they activated the phone tree and let everyone know the details of what the plan would be for Monday. It is now Monday; the staff and students are beside themselves with grief, and some are demanding that the sixteen-year-old be expelled from school.

SPEECH RIGHTS OF STUDENTS

1 In the auditorium today, students are making their speeches for student council. One honor student running for president has made the following speech:

> Hey Fellow Eagles, I am proud to announce my candidacy for the president of the Eagle Student Council. I would like to tell you about my concerns and promises that I will do my best to address when erected, I mean elected as your president. I promise to... And in closing, if you erect me, I mean elect me for president, I promise to make sure to get rid of some teachers that deserve to be fired. You know who I am talking about. Those of you who are sophomores and juniors have had to sustain the wrath from these worthless wastes of space. But rest assured, even if I have to create illusions, I will do what is necessary to get some teachers fired. (clapping and screaming from the crowd of students is almost deafening) Thank you and GO EAGLES!!!!

You were in the auditorium when the speech was being made, and you find it impossible to calm the students for several minutes. Students are so raucous that they start jumping over seats and running out of the auditorium into the school and parking lot.

2 A parent is in the front office at 7:15 a.m. wanting to talk about the letter that was sent home concerning the fifth grade graduation ceremony. The staff agreed with the members of the student council that ALL fifth graders wear Sunday dress for graduation. A letter conveying this desire, with examples of what Sunday dress looked like, was sent home yesterday. One mother argued that her daughter does not own a dress and would NOT come to graduation dressed as the school requested but as *she* desires. The mother has warned the staff that her daughter better not get in trouble for what she plans to wear. When asked what she is planning to wear, the mother scoffs, "You'll see on graduation

day." At graduation, the daughter comes in wearing a prom dress with a crown atop her head. This clearly does not meet the Sunday dress expectation.

3   Toots is an outspoken ninth grade student who follows the school rules and policies, but he also enjoys bucking the system. National presidential elections are nearing and, to prepare, the school district's discipline committee wrote a new rule and policy, which read in part, "No political T-shirts will be permitted." The new rule was sent home in a letter with the explanation that it would be enforced in three days. A week later, Toots has chosen to wear a political T-shirt three days in a row: One supporting the Republican Party, one supporting the Democrat Party, and one supporting the Independent Party. He believes that since he is not partisan to one party, the rule does not apply to him. He also tells you that his dad is a lawyer and will sue if you deny him his right to free speech and expression.

4   During lunchtime, students usually sit with like students. For example, the band students sit with one another, and the athletes sit with one another. Every day, one can witness different groups of students discussing religion. The most prominent religious groups on campus are the Seventh Day Adventists, Wickens, Catholics, Satanists, Baptists, and Mormons. Each group keeps to themselves, and their discussions are at an appropriate level. Praying is observed at times, along with holding hands and light singing. With the din from the cafeteria, each group's praying and singing is audible only when one is near them. A substitute teacher, who is also a parent at the school and an atheist, is appalled at what he witnesses. He believes no one should be allowed to practice any form of worship on school grounds. He goes to you to complain and expects you to stop the practice or he will sue.

RELIGION ON CAMPUS

1   Graduation is near, and a group of students have come to you asking for permission to say a prayer at the graduation ceremony. They show you what verses they would like to reference from their "bible" in the brief prayer that they have ready for your review. Although the prayer is non-denominational, you notice no reference to Jesus but many references to the universe and to the environment.

2   A teacher on your campus who is a part of a freshman team asks that her lunch period and her conference period be back to back each year so that she may pray and study her religious materials. This request is in conflict with her team's request for the conference period to be at the end of the day. The teacher has never agreed with

her team concerning the conference period and is close to suing the administrators, her team, and the school district for not honoring her religious needs.

3 A father sends a letter to school asking that his child be dismissed from saluting the American flag and saying the Pledge of Allegiance. He explains that honoring a graven image is against his family's religious beliefs. He also states in the letter that his child is not allowed to read anything that deals with war or hostilities, as their religion practices peace and love for all and is against war, violence, and fighting of any kind at any level.

PRIVACY

1 A group of students report to Mr. Kool that certain students have created a website that depicts him in a demeaning manner, and they ask permission to show him, on their i-Phones, the disparaging pictures and words. On the website, he finds

- his personal home phone number listed, which is an unlisted number;
- his mailing address listed;
- a picture of his home posted;
- a picture of his family posted;
- seemingly provocative pictures of him and another teacher on the campus posted; and
- a blog full of slanderous and false words written.

Mr. Kool takes the students to the administrator's office so that they can formally report the website through a written statement. Upon further investigation, you find that other teachers have webpages that were created and are linked through the school's website. This means that the school's website has been hacked and altered by someone other than a school or school district personnel.

2 A teacher, Mr. Talen, and a student, Bobby, have had personal differences since the beginning of the year. Bobby's parents visited with Mr. Talen and the administration at least twice and now have asked that Bobby be placed in a different classroom with a different teacher. The move occurs and, three weeks later, the parent's allege that Bobby came home stating that Mr. Talen told teachers on campus that he was a "jerk" and he always had "mommy swoop in to rescue him and save him from his responsibilities." The mother, being very livid, wrote the following e-mail to the administration stating,

Dear Administrator:

I would like to meet with you and Mr. Talen about some disparaging remarks that were made about my son Bobby to other educators in your building. Because Bobby is a child and a part of your school district, Mr. Talen had no right to speak of my son and of private matters concerning my son. He has violated FERPA (Family Educational Rights and Privacy Act), and I want to know what you will do about it. Please call or email me immediately to set a meeting.

Angry and dismayed,

Bobby's Mom

LIABILITY AND IMMUNITY

1 An "uncle" comes to the school to pick up his "niece," a seven-year-old first grader, around 1:30 p.m. He goes to the front office, tells the secretary that he is there to pick up his niece, and gives his name. The busy secretary does not check to see whether he is allowed to pick up the student and, when the student comes into the office smiling, she believes that the student knows the "uncle." At 3:30 p.m., the seven-year-old girl's mother calls and—panicked—tells that the bus just dropped off all the children who live in her neighborhood, but her daughter did not get off the bus. The mother is told that her uncle picked her up at 1:30 p.m. The mother explodes and says that she was to be released to only three people: the mother, the stepfather, and a female neighbor, all of which she explained in a letter that she personally submitted in writing to the school months ago. She calls the police to report her daughter missing.

2 A violent crime happens to a fourteen-year-old girl at your school. Another student (male), age sixteen, walked up to her during passing period and, from behind, slit her throat. He then calmly walked away and out of the school. Mayhem occurred as students screamed and ran to help the fourteen-year-old victim, who died at the scene. The police later apprehended the male student. The parents of the fourteen-year-old girl want to sue the school administrators and teachers for negligence, for lack of student discipline, for not having enough adults to supervise the halls, and for medical bills. The parents of the male student want to sue the school administrators and teachers for not appropriately implementing his IEP and for not preventing the heinous crime, even though the parents and educators knew he was emotionally disabled and diagnosed with a psychotic disorder.

3 Limbaugh High School is having their homecoming dance where ten teachers, four APs, two SROs, and five parent chaperones supervise about 1,000 students. As two teachers were passing the boy's bathroom, they heard moaning and screaming. When they entered the boy's bathroom, they saw a freshman male, fourteen years of age, having intercourse with a senior female, eighteen years of age. The freshman's parents have hired a lawyer and are suing the educators for allowing their son to be raped and not intervening quickly enough to prevent the rape. They will also press charges against the eighteen-year-old senior.

REFERENCES

Goren, P. (2012). Data, data, and more data—What's an educator to do? *American Journal of Education*, 118, 233–237.

Mandinach, E. (2012). A perfect time for data use: Using data-driven decision making to inform practice. *Educational Psychologist*, 47(2), 71–85.

Martin, A. (2011). Data-driven leadership. *School Library Monthly*, 28(2), 31–33.

Index